Khamr lays bare the close link of personal shame and failure, which are constants for us who were born and raised on the fringes of Cape Town. Framed through religion, this book is a living testimony that breaks down the walls of the insulated Coloured community. Leaving no stone unturned, Jamil F. Khan writes simply, with no airs and graces, but still manages to evoke deep emotion from the reader. This raw and honest account of his life enables Khan to present himself as a powerful yet vulnerable storyteller – a true revelation of a man who hurts, experiences trauma and stands tall in his vulnerability. While reading I found myself clutching the book to my chest as I took breaks to unpack, refocus and process the story.

Khamr tells of the Cape Malay community through the lens of those who don't fit in that is rooted in both privilege and pain. One can only expect intensive healing for the community from such a spectacular retelling of a lived experience. *Khamr* will leave you with a sense of gratitude to Khan for being allowed to see such a personal story, and to witness the triumph and resilience.
– Nadine Dirks, Gogo Magosha, writer, activist

With Khamr, *Jamil F. Khan has gifted us an exquisitely-crafted, ground-breaking memoir, destined to change and save lives. 'Coloured', Muslim and queer, Khan's coming-of-age story sketches the process of claiming an autonomous, fully actualised self as he grapples with classism, colourism and homophobia in a middle-class Cape Town 'Coloured' community, where appearances are everything.*

His turbulent journey includes navigating his father's alcoholism and the accompanying stigma that clings to the family – encapsulated in the slur 'waterslams' – and the destruction his father's addiction wreaks on his entire family, as well as the young boy's sense of security in the world. He understatedly sketches the constant undertow of homophobia, which threatens to entrench a sense of estrangement from his family and faith. Khan renders this excruciating journey into adulthood with elegant, moving prose, skilfully demonstrating the soul-destroying effects of intersecting oppression. Yet he leaves the reader with a sense of hope and redemption.

Unsparing and morally uncompromising, but full of compassion and empathy for the chief agents of his oppression, Khan succeeds in poignantly mapping his quest for a freedom that is ultimately revolutionary. He has documented an important, spirit-healing story; a beautiful undoing of some of the unspeakable violence of Black, queer erasure from history.
– BARBARA BOSWELL, ASSOCIATE PROFESSOR OF ENGLISH AT UCT, AND AUTHOR OF GRACE: A NOVEL

Khamr: The Makings of a Waterslams *is part memoir; part socio-political commentary. Jamil F. Khan, with unflinching honesty and searing vulnerability, speaks into the queer archival silence. He writes about us loudly. In the book, he reckons with becoming, substance abuse, familial hardships and notions of belonging at home and in a religion.*

This book gives us a space to reckon with our history of organised religion, sexual discrimination and the effects of colonialism on our lived experiences and histories. More importantly, this written text will speak to many Black Queer people and, may even, save lives. When I read this book I felt less alone, I felt seen in all my complexities and hidden histories.
– LETLHOGONOLO MOKGOROANE, CO-FOUNDER OF THE CHEEKY NATIVES

Family is our first true mirror. It is a constellation of complicated and interconnected forms of love and brutality. The searing, honest depiction of Jamil F. Khan's life story in Khamr *is like twisting a Rubik's cube to observe how race, patriarchy, addiction, language, class, queerness and religion interplay to create a uniquely South African experience that is of the present but also inextricably tied to our history as a nation. Khan takes the unbearable and passes it through a sieve of adult compassion and childhood innocence. What we are left with is a loving quilt of communal storms that produced one of the fiercest and most articulate thinkers of his generation.*
– LEBOGANG MASHILE, POET, AUTHOR, ACTRESS, PRODUCER

It is said 'we read to know we are not alone'. If this is indeed the case then this book, with each turn of the page, will make you feel like you have a very real confederate around every corner. It is rare that a writer is able to transport the reader to a consecrated space without it feeling like a peculiarly circuitous, if not bumptious journey. Khan has granted us privileged access to a candid recollection of social, political and personal events that shaped him as a human being.

It is also said that a story is a story is a story. But, let's face it, not everyone is compelling around a dinner table. Memories might be forever indelibly etched into our psyches, and we might all have the ability to recall them. However, it takes special skills like Khan's to know how parody and pathos are the yin and the yang of a good story, and the precision with which yarns need to be sutured with each delicate stitch.
– RAFIEK MAMMON, JOURNALIST AND THEATRE PRODUCER

Khamr

First published by Jacana Media (Pty) Ltd
First and second impression 2020

10 Orange Street
Sunnyside
Auckland Park 2092
South Africa
+2711 628 3200
www.jacana.co.za

© Jamil F. Khan, 2020

All rights reserved.

The financial assistance of the National Institute for the Humanities and Social Sciences (NIHSS) towards this publication is hereby acknowledged. Opinions expressed and those arrived at are those of the author and are not necessarily to be attributed to the NIHSS.

ISBN 978-1-4314-2979-0

Also available as an ebook.

Cover design by Maggie Davey
Photography by Antoine de Ras
Editing by Joey Kok
Proofreading by Megan Mance
Set in Sabon LT Std 10.5/15pt
Printed by ABC Press, Cape Town
Job no. 003665

See a complete list of Jacana titles at www.jacana.co.za

Khamr
The Makings of a Waterslams

Jamil F. Khan

For my ancestors who had their names taken and their tongues cut out.

For Mamma
For Pappa
For Mommy
For Daddy

We finally found the light. Rejoice, for the eternal night has lifted.

Contents

Foreword	xiii
Note to the reader	xvii
Part One: Waiting	1
Part Two: Sinking	79
Part Three: Revival	129
Epilogue	169
On Satan and god	179

Foreword

It is radical to say 'I count' in a world that constantly reminds you of your worthlessness. It is subversive to look at the systems of oppression that prop up that world and to insist 'I am here'. And when, to terrify you into silence, the ultimate counter-revolutionary cudgel 'What will people say?' is dragged out, it is revolutionary to say 'I don't give a fuck. This is my story, and everyone will hear it.'

One of the most radical acts of the 2011 Egyptian revolution came many months after those heady 18 days that were a magnet to people from around the world. In November 2011, a twenty-one-year-old Egyptian woman, Aliaa Elmahdy, turned the tables on our hypocrisy and sexual repression by undressing. She took a photo of herself standing in her parents' living room wearing nothing but stockings, red shoes, and a red hair clip. When she posted this photo on her blog, it was as if she'd thrown a Molotov cocktail from the barricades of the personal. Nakedness and sex, the very things that so exercise the patriarchy, became her weapons of political resistance. Our bodies, so often reduced to proxy battlefields in men's conflicts, can instead be turned into our weapons of choice.

Elmahdy's blog was flooded with visitors, and the vitriol against her came not just from religious conservatives incensed by female nudity but also from many liberals whom one would have expected to support her act. Instead, these liberals accused her of giving ammunition to the religious conservatives. As if clerics would ever run out of excuses for obsessing over women's bodies! And since when do revolutions allow their conservative opponents to set the agenda?

Some said it was not the time for Elmahdy's audacity. But what are revolutions if not audacious? Some said that her photo would sway Egyptians against the revolution by making them think that it was indeed composed of young men and women doing drugs and having sex in tents in Tahrir Square, as the regime's media claimed. But it is the job of a revolution to shock, to provoke and to upset, not to behave or to be polite.

Some complained that Elmahdy's body was unattractive by Egyptian standards of beauty: that she was not curvy enough and that she had not shaved her pubic hair and so on. It's laughable that some men want even those women breaking social taboos to fit into their mold of attractive desirability.

Far from being the immature naif some have tried to paint her as, Elmahdy found the soft underbelly of our hypocrisy – and she kicked. She wrote on her blog: 'Put on trial the artists' models who posed nude for art schools until the early 70s, hide the art books and destroy the nude statues of antiquity, then undress and stand before a mirror and burn your bodies that you despise to forever rid yourselves of your sexual hangups before you direct your humiliation and chauvinism and dare to try to deny me my freedom of expression.'

Elmahdy received the inevitable death threats and had to leave for Sweden. An Egyptian lawyer filed a motion to have her stripped of her Egyptian nationality, a case that did not go anywhere but that gives you an idea of how much outrage her act generated. All this woman did was take off her clothes in her parents' living room and post a picture of it! You had to go to her blog to see it. She did not stage a naked protest in the street. Tellingly, Elmahdy received more vitriol than has ever been mustered against the sexual violence that plagues girls and women in Egypt.

In this memoir of radical truth and honesty, Jamil F. Khan has also stripped. He too takes us into his parents' living room where he blows up politeness and its twin, silence. He demands you look and he refuses to let go of your gaze, as he peels back layers of artifice. The more he removes, the more he insists you bear witness to his courage. It is a courage that spares no one, including himself.

As a gay Coloured man of Muslim descent, Jamil F. Khan knows intimately the multiple tentacles of oppression his identities leave him vulnerable to. In reckoning with each of his identities, Jamil knows the power of presenting what is rarely centred. A hierarchy of visibility and priority has long favoured white voices over those of colour, even when those voices are queer. In presenting the ways he has defied, disobeyed and disrupted, Jamil models for others a way to create a life that he had never thought possible but which now looks attainable for a reader who once thought they were alone in their fight to be free.

Family, school, mosque, university, friends, lovers: Nothing and no one is spared in Jamil's fight to be free. Are you uncomfortable? Revolutions are not meant to be comfortable. Are you outraged? Who said revolutions were anything *but* outrageous?

The revolution in South Africa, which came many years before the revolution in Egypt, must continue to reckon with a question that many uprisings, everywhere, too often shirk: Who was the revolution for?

If the revolution is simply a cisgender dick swinging contest between one group of heterosexual men against another so that the former can have a bit more of the latter's power, then it was never for all of us. Where is the revolution for those who are not cis or who are not any of the identities that place you at the apex of the white supremacist, capitalist, heteropatriarchy?

When you dare to challenge those systems of oppression, you will hear 'Who do you think you are?'

It is revolutionary to say 'I am the one whose stories you can no longer silence. And my stories will be your fucking end.'

That is what Jamil F. Khan has done in these pages.

Mona Eltahawy, Egyptian-American journalist and author of *Headscarves and Hymens*, and *The Seven Necessary Sins for Women and Girls*

Note to the reader

When asked where I am from, I hesitate to say Cape Town. It is both geographically and politically incorrect for me to say that. Where I grew up, I could not see the outline of Table Mountain clearly or smell the icy waft of the Atlantic Ocean. None of what people see when they imagine Cape Town was within my reach. I grew up where the dry heat of summer ricocheted off finely powdered sand, hospitable to only the most resilient foliage.

Where we were, nobody cared to write reviews for publication in a brochure. I, too, am but a visitor to Cape Town, and it tolerates me for only as long as is necessary. In reality, it's not at all the welcoming natural wonder we claim it to be. The ocean is glacial, the streets are claustrophobic, and the air is filled with the anger of ancestors long since removed from their rightful homes. Cape Town is a city of open secrets – dirty secrets. That may be one attribute I can identify with.

I cannot lie and say that writing this book has been a joyful experience. It has been daunting, to say the least. Most notably, it has been an eerie experience in which art imitated life. The writing process found itself plagued and impeded by many of the same oppressive and restrictive conditions it sought to describe. The task of excavating history seems linear enough. Accessing memories in a form of internal time travel should be simple. It can be, but when that process is accompanied by the living recreation of its own subject matter something incredible happens. Every word that followed revealed itself at the appropriate time in an attempt to save me from the present. Under the ever-present threat of freezing up and shutting down, I was stolen away by this story that would not rest any longer.

There is something to be said for the conditions under which writing occurs and how responsive the words are to their surroundings. Though it was an agonising process for me, I am happy that I wrote this book in surroundings that were reminiscent of my upbringing.

The past is a continuum. It morphs and moults, but it remains immortal. The past lives in us and dies when we die if we don't pass it on. The past I was reliving while writing this book is my familial inheritance. Writing sent me back and forth between a beginning and an end, sometimes indistinguishable in my memory; the cycle of trauma narrated here has been hard to quell. It is also through words that we, as a family, have willed this inheritance of abuse to end, but words alone mock our efforts.

This story is my ultimate attempt at an end. Maybe if the words are employed to travel beyond the no man's land of the promises we make to each other, they will take up the offer to work. When we utter them under our dishonest breaths, they are too easily retracted and forgotten when they need something to bind them with. We need something to bind us with.

Maybe the heat of the ink as it is seared onto the paper might demand some kind of commitment from us. Maybe the bright light of outsider eyes will betray our commitment to secrecy just one last time and enough to stop the boomerang.

For me, this is an end, and this story will never have to be told anew again. For those still weighed down by the injustice of generational shame, this is meant to be a beginning.

We deserve every chance to be remembered.

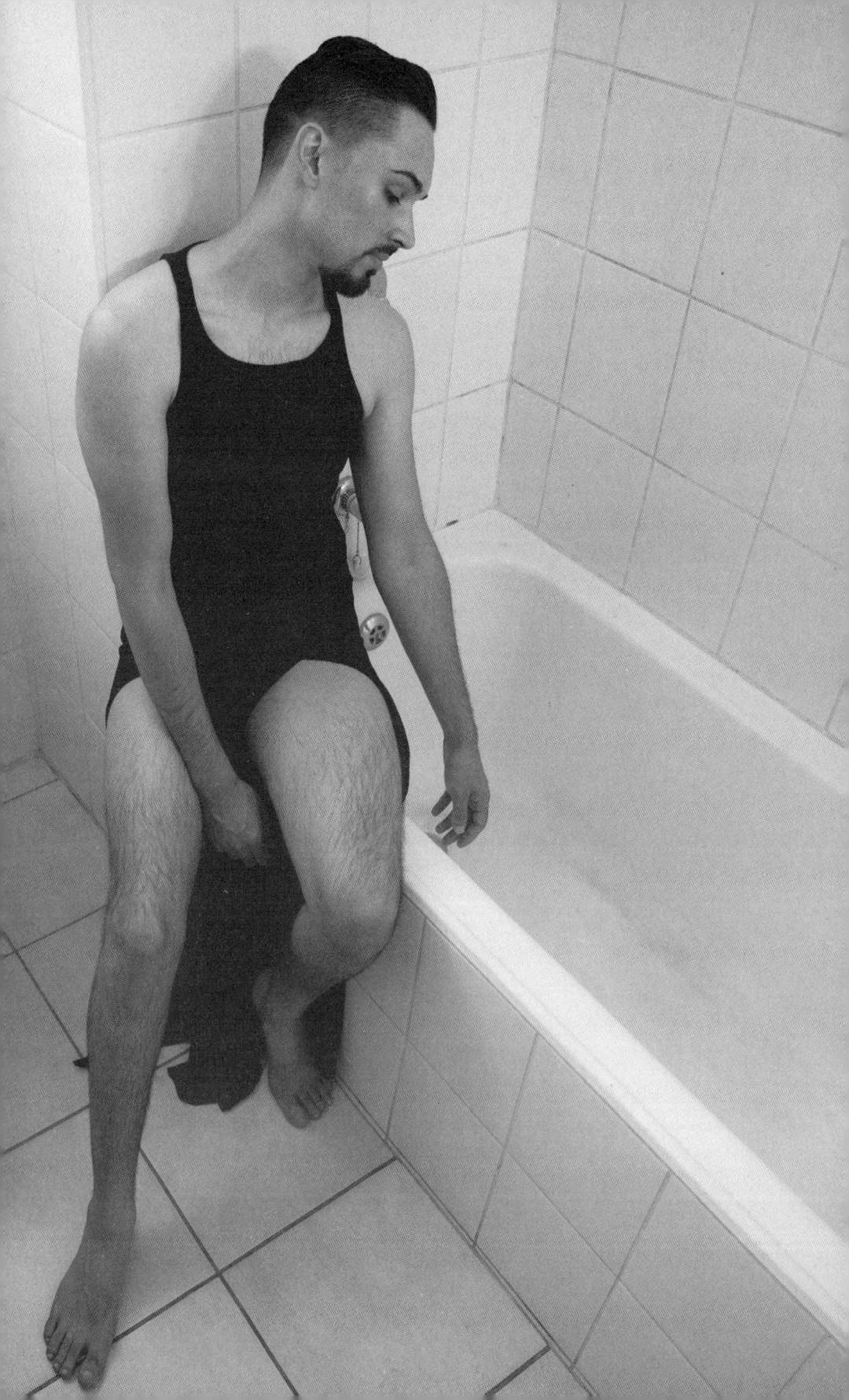

PART I
WAITING

One

My loneliest moment arrived more unexpectedly than my four-year-old imagination could conceive. I was pacing the perimeter of the hole in our backyard where the new swimming pool would go. It was one of those days where the sky was such a crystal hue of blue, staring at it long enough might have lifted you off the ground and caused you to float in the space between heaven and earth, as the good books teach. The earth was dry and, worse, the soil where we lived had a strange relationship with water, which rolled off it, like oil, so not even the prospect of watering could make a difference. Walking through it barefoot, I always kicked up a fine black dust, which settled between my toes and seemed to cling to my skin. Barefoot, I walked around with feet resembling black and brown marbled rock formations on most days. Perhaps it was a metaphor for many stubborn relationships I would witness around me, because, though we all needed each other, nourishing each other proved difficult.

Danger to a four-year-old is like Greek mythology – always something that other people worry about. Until then, the earth had always stayed steady under my feet, even if it were only to teach me respect for gravity.

Counting my steps around the edge of the hole provided solace for the chaos happening inside the house. I was a very contained child, though not stunted. My imagination was always a refuge, an unseen world where I could live freely. A world where I wasn't hiding from the policing of adults, the cruelty of prejudiced children or a fear of the ever-present danger of difference, which follows people like me to their graves.

I didn't feel the fall, but my view had changed suddenly. A mountain of deep brown earth eclipsed my view of the house, and the Vibracrete walls that enclosed the backyard grew much taller than they were a few seconds before. It was the closest I've ever come to having the earth swallow me. If the nagging fear of violence that marginalised people often experience manifested in physical form, that fall might have been it. It is something we are always guarding against, trying to circle it as skilfully as we know how, but every now and then, the earth shifts, and our worlds turn upside down. Nothing looks familiar anymore and, for many, recovery just isn't possible. Maybe this too was a representation of the lives we live – one way in, and rarely any way out.

I had fallen into the hole. I doubt that I knew what was happening to me, but I quickly realised I had to get out. I was not concerned for my safety as much as I was petrified of being shouted at for getting sand on myself. Cleanliness was at all times important; after all, we were always a representation of our homes and communities. One speck of dust or unruly curl that managed to escape the grip of a hair clip could bring the entire community's value system into question.

Looking around the canyon of dirt, I took a few moments before I buckled under the weight of the realisation that it may be the end of my life as I knew it. Facing the possibility, I had to try and get myself out as quietly and neatly as possible. I grasped at the fine roots sticking out of the earth as if they were ropes. To my eyes, they seemed strong enough to help me jungle-gym my way out.

With each failed attempt to lift myself out of the sunken ground, I grew more desperate. How was I going to get out of this and clean myself up without anyone noticing?

Nobody knew I was there. What felt like hours had passed, and I finally started giving up. Panic set in, and I let out a quiet self-deprecating cry. My cries grew louder until I was completely unhinged. The feeling of resignation to circumstance can be freeing but, to a petrified child, it only means death. Having to experience such panic without a single caregiver in sight, or the prospect of help arriving, is the most harrowing form of abandonment I know. Fear with protection is unsettling, but without, it is annihilation.

I suspect my cries alerted my parents and the neighbours, who were having a little party in the house, to my distress. My mother recalls how my father swiftly jumped in and took me out, with the assistance of our neighbours. The moment at which I was discovered and lifted out of the hole escapes my memory. The panic and sheer terror of the moment made it very difficult for me to experience what was happening in any meaningful way. We are known to block out trauma that weighs heavier than we are able to hold – I do remember that the experience was *that* terrifying to me. I believed I was going to die – an idea too immense for adults to confront, what still for a child?

One neighbour, Aunty Mirrie, took me and put me in the bathtub. I could not understand why I had to be rinsed with cold water. That was possibly more traumatic than falling into the hole. A blur of faces zoomed past me as I, the object of everyone's concern, was retroactively coddled by the guilt of jubilant adults shocked into partial sobriety at the prospect of my near death. The rest of the day went quiet.

My first memorable encounter with danger was to prepare me for a life of peril. The perpetual pattern of being closed in on started here. Despite the efforts at protecting me from the cruelty of the world, the home my parents created was often my first encounter with danger. Our house, in the early years of my life, was the lekker huis or fun house in the neighbourhood. Coloured neighbourhoods in Cape Town, no matter their spatial arrangements, all had an incestuous sense of community. Everyone was so deeply enmeshed with the lives of their neighbours, and where some formed friendships, others formed news forums. Whatever the setup, there was always an attempt at integration that enabled intimate involvement with the lives of others, or at the very least a steady flow of second-hand information.

The intention behind this form of social organisation was in and of itself not malicious, even if it sometimes resulted in harm. We often found ourselves clinging to each other in our respective neighbourhoods based on our shared sense of grief stemming from displacement. Everyone in the road was from somewhere else. Somewhere more beautiful.

My father would often talk about his upbringing in Paarl and Oakdale, where there were lush, rolling hills and vineyards aplenty. My grandfather owned property and a convenience store in Paarl – later a house in Oakdale – and my father would often recall playing in the peach and pomegranate orchards in the backyard. He conjured images of vastness and summer emotions drifting through the air. Our parents knew what it was like to taste the fruits of their land, once. The life he described, although also turbulent because of his parents, was pleasant and carefree through the eyes of the child he once was. When those areas were later declared white, my family was removed in a most inhumane fashion. According to my father's version of events, my grandfather came home to find a pile of rubble where their home once was. Devastated and bewildered, my grandfather asked the white 'bystanders' in hard hats watching his despair with callous amusement what had happened to his house. The response was something to be expected of a psychopath: 'Huis, Meneer? Hier was nooit 'n huis nie.' Although this tragedy did not drop his family into abject poverty, as it did many others, the sense of displacement certainly characterised my father's sense of self. It could be seen in the way he and my mother considered our home, the first one they could call their own, as a badge of honour.

Nostalgia for a different home always appeared in conversations. Recollections of happier, more secure times peppered general conversation, like it was a key ingredient in anchoring us to the present we begrudgingly found ourselves in: a community of vastly different people tied together by a shared history of displacement and violence and a contrived sense of relation born out of shared cultural practices and the loss thereof.

That was life in Bernadino Heights – a suburb in Kraaifontein, far flung from the pristine postcard aesthetic of Cape Town. The Northern Suburbs – affectionately termed 'behind the boerewors curtain', as an obvious reference to Afrikaner cultural hegemony – was a strange place. Its strangeness was also the constitutive other of the Southern Suburbs, which was closer to the city centre where the melting pot of cultures metaphorically resided. As Muslim people, our religious and cultural preservation depended on exchanges with other Muslim people who were found mostly in the Southern Suburbs and on the Cape Flats. Moving away also took us away from the community influences meant to keep us in line. Wedged between the white suburban prowess of Durbanville and the neatly zoned farming wealth of Stellenbosch, we were somewhat comfortable.

Our house at 4 Broadway Crescent was the first on the left or the last on the right, depending on which side you entered the crescent. My father financed the house in 1988, with a bit of help from a senior colleague who gave him the deposit to approach the bank at the time. It was what my mother described as her dream home. Being able finally to say it was her very own meant more to her than any architectural or other 'selling points' ever would. She would always say: 'I thought I finally found my white picket fence life. I was going to be like the women on *Dynasty*. That was my dream house!' It was spacious, by the standards of the times, with a garden that stretched around the house. The pathway leading to the door was paved with beige bricks and lined with rose bushes, interrupted only by a white post box, a painted wooden barrel nailed horizontally to a tree stump.

The entrance was adjacent to a generous, carpeted lounge that wrapped around to the open-plan dining area and kitchen counter. A passage separated the house into front and back, with bedrooms in the order of my sister Tayshira, me and my parents on the left, and the kitchen, toilet and bathroom on the right. My room was sufficient but awkwardly cramped. As a labour of love, my mother's father, who was a carpenter by profession, built me a wardrobe that covered the short wall flanking the passage and above the door. Made of chipboard, it was covered in white melamine and adorned with blue and yellow handles to match the carpet and vertical blinds. The colour scheme was all my choice. Though not the best, it might have been an early manifestation of my propensity for making bold choices. Directly across from the door was a nook with a bookshelf and desk in the same style as the wardrobe. My bed stood by the window. A single foam mattress could hardly fit between my bookshelf and my bed – but it was my space. My sister's room was the mirror image of mine, and also where I wanted to spend most of my time as younger siblings do. When I got older, I appreciated my room as a haven, mostly to escape my father's drunken nagging.

My father worked in textiles, as what he referred to as a textile engineer. He sold textile auxiliaries to dye houses and textile treatment plants and consulted them, troubleshooting when the chemistry of the fabric treatments went awry. He studied textile science in Germany in the '70s and learnt to speak German fluently. In the late-'80s he started working for Rudolf Chemicals – a German multinational company. The textile industry in the Western Cape was a lifeline for Coloured people, who made up a large proportion of pattern makers, seamstresses, salespeople and managers. My father had the loyalty and camaraderie of nearly all the Coloured dye house managers in the palm of his hand. They made a point of buying his products, perhaps exclusively to give him the upper hand on his white competitors. Ironically, the profits went back to white Germans, but if it meant that he exceeded his targets, his clients considered it a victory, at least for his image. They also knew that when they found themselves in a predicament of any kind, they could call on him. He was somewhat of a surrogate boss to them. With their support, he was one of the highest-selling players in the Western Cape textile industry. A blessing and a curse.

After working for a few years, my father was promoted to director – a position with only the benefit of social currency, but nothing material that he could own. His new position came with a company car: a black Mercedes-Benz E220, an expense account for entertaining international clients (and us) – and an inflated ego.

In 1994, he took a second bond on our house to pay for renovations. Ours became one of the most ostentatious houses in the crescent, with tiled bathroom and kitchen walls, shower doors where most had curtains, an aluminium front door and windows with white aluminium roller shutters and an automated garage door.

To Coloured people, the statement that material luxury made was profound. Many of the people in our crescent lived modest lives with little to flash about. To everyone else we were rich. The presence of my father's perceived wealth made quite a stir in the neighbourhood, but also set us on a collision course with a precarious middle-class illusion.

At our house, everything flowed in abundance and attracted anyone in the road who was looking for a good time or just a place to bond with the neighbours. Our opposite neighbours, Aunty Mirrie and Uncle Bobby, regularly popped over for drinks, less for socialising and recreation and more to escape a banal reality and a general sense of discomfort with life, although the two bled into each other. Mrs Raikes, who lived next to us, completed the main clique. When there was a booze-up, these three neighbours were always at the house.

There was nothing extraordinary about this – except that we were the only Muslim people on our crescent. Anybody who knows – not only Muslim people, but also those living in Cape Town – will tell you that the biggest embarrassment to Cape Muslims is drunkenness. More so than drug abuse, which cannot always be detected in someone's behaviour or seen in their appearance. It is generally about what can be seen and attract judgement, not what is right according to the scripture.

Khamr (wine or intoxicants) is strictly forbidden, as it leads to the alteration of senses and defiles the body, according to the Qur'an. A good Muslim cannot practise Islam under the influence of alcohol. We have a name for such Muslims; we call them Waterslamse. The 'slams' is derived from Islam and ascribed to followers of Islam. Diluted not only in practice but also in faith, Waterslamse don't deserve the respect the pious Muslims do. Neither from Muslims nor any other religious community.

In popular Coloured discourse, the figure of the Waterslams presents a complex interrelationship between respectability, religious superiority, prejudicial solidarity, power and shame. For many of us, image is all we have. How others perceive you determines much of how you live your life, and falling out of favour with the community can have devastating consequences, because there is no home for you elsewhere. Historically, we also had very little to hold on to besides our faith, which served to forge a sense of community – even between those who believed differently. So, the commonly understood rules of religious practice serve as a law for everyone, Muslim and Christian, to abide by. Although believers all believe their way is the only pathway to heaven, the only thing worse than 'the other faith' was poor faith – or no faith at all. That was us, those of poor faith, the Waterslamse who could not be bound by the rules. As products of social conditioning, we do love wielding hypothetical power over others, even if it is only through our scornful looks and snide comments. Though we did not experience this judgement overtly in our immediate community, it was always in the air.

Both my parents drank in the early years of my childhood. Neither had any appreciation for moderation, which fuelled every weekend's festivities into a raucous party. Many mornings after the party my mother would call either Aunty Mirrie or Mrs Raikes to ask if my sister and I were at their houses, because she could not remember anything. Luckily, in those days, neighbours raised the community's children together. Leaving us in the care of equally drunk neighbours may have been reckless, but still, it was safer than the chaos being had in our house.

Every party would always start out festive. As the adults started unwinding and feeling less burdened by the reality of everyday drudgery, Mrs Raikes's granddaughter Sue-Nashley (affectionately known as Nessie) and I would play in the setting sun. Sometimes our other neighbours Uncle Malcolm and Aunty Cheryl and their daughter Chandré would join us. My sister Tayshira would hang out with the older children, like Aunty Mirrie's daughter Jackie and Nessie's sister Liezel. Every now and then we would run into the house for some snacks or drinks before darting out again.

When dusk fell, we were ushered inside the house by our own fears of abduction. By this time, we waded through a forest of adults who were swaying. Everyone's face had taken on a different form, slightly distorted and almost vacant. It seemed like a worship ritual or a séance through which they hoped to conjure up a god who actually cared. Or maybe it was to find an alternative to the god who never showed up. It was chilling to watch the people at the centre of your world perform such joyous helplessness, because if they were seeking help elsewhere, where would yours come from? Being alienated from your most trusted ally can only make you resent the source of the alienation and, as time passed, I became resentful. The sight of alcohol would evoke a visceral fear in me, because I began to associate it with abandonment and loss. I was resentful towards alcohol, those who consumed it and those who stood by and did nothing to stop the disaster it always caused.

The night grew deeper, and fatigue eventually set in from a long day of playing. Finding my parents in my own home became more and more difficult. Drunk adults have little time for the needs of uncomfortable children while in the thick of a party. Protocol would be to find the most lucid adult, usually Aunty Mirrie, and get the best care possible. Sometimes Tayshira was a good second best.

When sunrise came, the luck of the draw placed me in one or other Christmas bed at a neighbour's house – something that felt festive as well. Waking up on a mattress at my friend's house somewhat erased the trauma of trying to get my mother's attention to no avail, although it could still be traced on my morning face. A four-year-old has no frame of reference for their circumstances and, to me, this was just life. I did not realise at the time that I was having sleepovers for a reason other than my own desire for fun with my friends. Years later, conversations with Tayshira revealed the reality, but there was nothing to regret. In casual conversation with my mother, recalling our childhood she said: 'Remember how we would wake up at the neighbours, and Mommy and Daddy didn't know where we were?' My mother corroborated her version of events with: 'Yes, that was terrible. I had to phone and ask Mrs Raikes or Mirrie if my children are with them.' I did not escape unscathed, despite now understanding the position my parents found themselves in.

Children have long memories, but not for the bad things. *That* we store for adulthood. What seems like the end of the world for a child can quickly be turned around with some sort of distraction, but the traumas that really do end our worlds often overstay.

My early childhood was an odd existence. I had so much to navigate with such a small body. I know now that I was in need of vocabularies I would not encounter for years. In a world of total contradiction, adults were my only anchor, even if they were the contradictions. I may not have had much of a need for sense making at the time, but I knew that this is not how people should live. I knew that not being able to find my parents in my own home was not how other people live.

Seeing my parents change like werewolves before my eyes nearly every weekend taught me early on that nobody is who you think they are. People change, and there is nothing you can do about it. I learnt that you can find a home nowhere but in yourself. I am yet to apply the lesson, since I still try and be a home to others. Apparently the children of substance abusers have two potential fates: to fall into the same cycle of dysfunction, or to become overachievers often recognised for their strength, resilience and a keen interest in housing injured beings in one form or another. I have become an exceptionally strong person with a highly developed sense of intuition. Like my father, I am also Farouk – it's my second name – which in Arabic means the one who distinguishes truth from falsehood. My father did not seem to honour his name, but in fairness, he was dragging a legacy of weight behind him, requiring a different kind of strength.

In any form, strength born from trauma is an unnecessary burden.

Two

Mrs Sophie Raikes was quite short, a wide-set woman with dark skin and short grey hair. She mostly wore skirts and dresses. In those days, fashion sense was often dictated by a combination of respectability and body politics that required any woman who was not a model size to cover her curves. There were times when Mrs Raikes couldn't be bothered and waltzed down the road in fleece tracksuit pants and a beanie – she had nobody to prove herself to.

Since I could remember, she was wrinkly, though she was not much older than my father, who had just turned 45 when I was born. It is interesting how different their lives were. At the time my father welcomed me – his third child, from his second marriage – into the world, Mrs Raikes had already welcomed multiple grandchildren, who were, by that time, older than Tayshira. I would later come to understand the gauntlet she ran to earn her wrinkles. She hailed from De Doorns, a farming town in the Hex River Valley of the Western Cape, though she had also lived in Paarl before settling in Kraaifontein.

Like most women of her time, she had settled down with a husband: Fred, or 'Small' as we knew him. But Sophie Raikes was not the kind of woman to take what she got and just be happy with it. So, the marriage lasted as long as it suited her, and she divorced after what I imagine were multiple attempts to hold on and save the sacred commitment. Her new husband, Maurice Raikes, coincidentally a friend of my father's, was a wealthy Coloured man. He was the owner of Raikes Removals. He bought the house at 6 Broadway for cash and set Mrs Raikes up comfortably. The only condition was that she was not to have contact with her family again, except for one daughter he had taken a liking to. There Mrs Raikes was, living a solitary life as a trophy wife without the laughter of her children.

I've often wondered what it must be like to make such an impossible choice. It is ironic that we live in a world that values individuality and choice so much, because for many, every day is an attempt at navigating the impossible and choosing life over every other instinct that helps us makes sense of living. For Coloured women, in fact all Black women, this is especially true. I wonder what could have become of Mrs Raikes, had she not been born into such a brutally oppressive and restrictive life so many Black people endure today still.

Shortly after they moved in, Mr Raikes died. Mrs Raikes was known as the neighbourhood gossip, but she was evidently not the only one. Rumour, as designed by the opposite neighbour Mrs K, had it that Mr Raikes's death was mysterious. Mrs K believed Mrs Raikes poisoned her husband, so that she could inherit his wealth. 'I'm telling you, Mrs Khan, she poisoned that man. The one day he was standing in the driveway, healthy as a horse, and the next day he was dead. Tell me that doesn't sound suspicious to you?' she would say to my mother. The taken-for-granted, incestuous sense of community in Coloured areas ensured that those who did not allow the jury into their lives paid dearly through the suspicions attached to them. This is how malicious the need to monitor and foster communal lives could get.

If she indeed heard the rumour, such an accusation must have hurt Mrs Raikes. Little else is known, but Mrs Raikes kept the house, sold the car before her stepson could take it, since he was apparently fighting tooth and nail to keep her from inheriting her late husband's assets – and welcomed all her daughters and their children home.

Around the same time, word from Paarl was that Small was descending into alcoholism and had started living on the streets. The ease with which something like that could happen for working-class Coloured people is still alarming. Class is a tightrope in Coloured communities, and everyone is watching. Even the slightest misstep could mean the severest descent. It is brutal.

At the behest of her children, Mrs Raikes allowed Small to come and live with them – on condition that he become the house runner and resident handyman, or so it was said. I think this may have been exaggerated, because nobody could understand the optics in such patriarchal utopia. There had to be an explanation for Small doing things like running the house, which was considered women's work. The most plausible explanation would be that he did it voluntarily, as a contribution to the household, since he was the recipient of such generous hospitality.

I didn't know it at the time, but she was the first visible feminist I encountered. Sophie Raikes owned and headed her own household, where she made the rules. She made her own choices and enabled her daughters to make theirs in a world that reflected nothing but male domination to them. In our street, apart from one widow, she was the only woman who did not live under the rule of a man in the traditional nuclear family structure. Though the circumstances of her independence were not directly of her making, her life was hers – and it showed. Men related to her differently. They had no choice, since she was not merely the extension of a man, whom they would usually extend respect to first. She was there on their level, mostly a level above, since she had no bond repayments to work for, while they still aspired to own their properties. The influence of ownership and providence on a man's self-esteem is not to be underestimated. Mrs Raikes had no time for it – she owned not only her house but her identity, which were closely linked.

AT HOME, WE WERE PREPARING for yet another party. The early years of my childhood entailed many celebrations, and I recall the merriment of the first democratic elections distinctly. Everyone was so happy. This party was different, yet it still followed a familiar script. It seemed like every day was a party around that dwindling summer of 1994. Everyone was genuinely happy at the possibilities they imagined democracy would enable for them. My mother was ready to move into her house in Camps Bay. Others expressed similar articulations of material and spatial justice, which was really a yearning for ease and comfort in their lives. A life free from the worry of the next pay cheque, the never-ending cycle of aspiration and consumption, and the opportunity to live instead of surviving. This, I think, is what many Black people imagined the end of apartheid to mean. For some, justice never comes.

More and more people started streaming through the door, and the buzz of clashing voices filled my head. As each couple entered, their children would be ushered swiftly into my room, where we were all gathered, like coats at a nightclub entrance. My cramped room became even smaller; we must have looked like a cast of crabs teeming in a bucket. My memory of such occasions contradicts what we think of as remembering, because the details swirl within a larger blur.

I already knew what was coming. Whenever there was a party, I experienced a certain kind of dissociation, because although I was happy that there would be food and fun, I also knew I would lose my parents to the occasion. I mourned the loss of my mother more than my father. In those days, mothers were mostly exclusively nurturers and caretakers, and fathers were breadwinners. Even when women were breadwinners or equal contributors, the dynamics of most homes still conformed to the performance of traditional gender roles, which revolved around stroking a man's ego. In our home, my mother was the nurturer and caregiver.

When sober, my mother was the most perfect thing to me. There was nothing in the world I needed more. She responded to every need I had and even anticipated some. She was besotted with me, and I with her. We were the best of friends. When she was drunk, the grief I felt was akin to what one probably feels when death descends. Completely unrecognisable to me, the woman who was using her body had no care for me. I never mattered less in my life than I did to my drunk mother. There was neither time nor space to consider that at the party. There's an old saying that goes: 'Children should be seen and not heard', which really meant to put a gag on the honesty of children in the presence of adult fuckery. They told us that as a way to escape accountability for the double standards they practised in trying to raise us with values they knew were a rouse. When the good times rolled in our house, children were neither seen nor heard. It was our introduction to invisibility in the harshest way. It was as if someone flipped a switch on our reality, turning it off. I realise now that they also needed an escape from the drudgery of emulating white suburbia, even if we were the casualties of the scam.

Dancing and singing must have sent vibrations to the top of the street by the time the party got into the messier part of the evening. People had started losing their senses and their regard for our home. One of the things I hated most about these times was that I stopped feeling at home in my own space. Strangers suddenly had more access to space and belonging than I had. I had never felt lonely before this realisation. I wanted to run away and find a nice family that didn't turn into werewolves when the moon came out. I wanted to find a place where adults always made me feel safe and where there were no operating hours attached to parenting. Hollywood really did a great job portraying even animals as compliant with the rules of nuclear family structures, which were reliable and consistent. What shame to face reality where none of that played out against the backdrop of some dizzy theme song about the infallibility of love. There in Kraaifontein, we knew love by a different name, and it did not always appreciate being called.

Mrs Raikes was hovering around the kitchen counter trying to get onto a white faux-leather high-back barstool. The seat was at the level of my four-year-old neck, requiring good balance for anyone to mount it. The Elvis Presley CDs had just come out. She had a paper plate with some potjiekos and rice, as by this time everybody was trying to eat something to bind their battered stomach linings. Trying to scoop herself onto the chair proved futile, a couple of times. In fairness, it took presence of mind and coordination, even for a sober person, to comfortably mount that chair, so doing it while drunk must have warranted the summoning of quite a few gods known to humankind. To gain some balance, she put the plate down and made a final attempt. With a jump and a sway, she made it, which was half the battle.

Reaching for her plate sent her hurtling forward into the counter, but she stabilised herself. As she grabbed her plate to bring it closer, her altered agreement with gravity betrayed her, and she threw herself too far back. Behind her, the party was none the wiser to her predicament. At this point it was not only children who were unseen; most of the party goers were in a stupor of varying intensities. With a last attempt to either crash back into the counter or abandon the plate to grab the counter, all systems failed, and with a cry for help to my mother, who had appeared a few steps away, Mrs Raikes exclaimed, 'Khan!', before free falling backwards with her plate of potjiekos. Meat, rice and carrots covered her face and the plush cream lounge carpet. That carpet bore the brunt of every party, which served it everything from vomit to cigarette ash regularly.

Someone hurried to get her back to her feet, with great effort. Luckily he saw her, because few people were lucid or capable enough to help her. One consolation may have been that at that level of intoxication, emotions like shame and embarrassment tend to self-destruct, and Mrs Raikes was left only with a logistical quandary to consider. For some reason, drunk people who have lost control of their legs become 10 times heavier than they usually are.

It was probably Aunty Mirrie who cleaned up the mess. She always managed to keep herself together and could often be seen cleaning up, tending to the children or popping out to get more alcohol. If there was one person who could be admired in all the mess, it was Miriam Carelse. I had never seen someone handle their liquor the way she did. I don't know if it was because she just didn't drink as much, or as fast as the rest, or because her body was set up differently, but it would always take the longest for her to lose herself to alcohol. So, she would always be hovering around with a keen sense of duty to keep everything as orderly as possible.

No sooner had the commotion passed than everybody was twisting and jiving to the sounds of Elvis Presley – one of my mother's favourite singers and what would become a constant trigger for my own feelings of abandonment. To this day, Elvis Presley's music reminds me of being motherless in my own home. The sound of his voice inspires feelings of insecurity and conjures images of sadness and darkness. For years, I would believe my mother was trying to taunt me by playing his music, because I could not separate it from this context. I still cringe when I hear it. By the time 'Kiss Me Quick' came on, the imminent end of the party was signalled. Most people had left, and those who stayed behind were either passed out somewhere or highly incoherent. It was like a scene out of a zombie movie.

When the music stopped, my ears were pierced by the sound of a thousand glass harps being played at the same time. I was delirious with fatigue but still hopeful that my mother would return to me in a form I recognised. Everything was slightly fuzzy, and I could not find the feeling of home. The only people I could rely on were in need of care themselves, and this was perhaps the start of the cycle of dysfunction so many Black children inherit from parents who abuse substances to escape the trauma of a brutal history of apartheid violence, which still controls them today. There was nothing left but my parents and the misery of a good time's ghost.

My mother, who by now had offended everyone, turned her attention to my father. She was an angry, wild drunk. There was a deep-seated violence that would always come out of her when she drank. Insecurity was my mother's constant companion, always following the many versions of personhood she expressed at any time. I would later come to learn why this was so, but when viewing her through the eyes of a child who just needed protection from the world, I only saw a monster.

At the time she could not drive, and in her cantankerous intoxication started badgering my father about why he won't give her a car. This was her go-to trouble starter every time they drank. It was not only because she didn't know how to operate a car, but also because my father didn't trust her to stay sober and be responsible with his purchase, even if he was not. He would not admit it, but he probably couldn't afford to buy her a car anyway. Somewhat more sober, he tried to reason with her, but my mother was not the type of person to hear anything when drunk. He walked away to create some distance between them, probably hoping she would retreat, since he thwarted her attempts at confrontation, but she was not the kind of person to let her grievance go, valid or not. My mother, taking advantage of the fact that he had turned his attention away from her, crouched and crawled towards him. It was like watching a scene from a *National Geographic* special, where a jaguar was stalking its prey. She had an intent scowl on her face, almost knowing that her target was locked, and she was directed precisely at his ankles. He was not at all suspicious of the silence that suddenly befell her and probably hoped that she had relented. But, with quiet skill, she grabbed his leg and bit him. My father jumped like a gazelle escaping the jaws of impending death.

I burst into tears, as children often do at the sight of violence, and my father called me towards him. 'Kyk nou wat doen jy, Farieda!'

Despite his attempts at instilling some guilt in her for causing my hysteria, my mother seemed to have no concern for my distress. She continued to argue and fight.

There would be many more such fights, until she got her car. It might have been the day she threw a TV at my father that alerted him to the seriousness of her request.

Discord and unrest would remain a consistent feature of my home life, even though the optics changed. Alcohol abuse and the dysfunction it caused shaped my life irrevocably. The burden of adulthood descended on me way too soon, as my parents hammered through their relationship with each other, which danced to the tune of their own traumas.

My mother admittedly didn't take kindly to marriage. On the eve of her wedding, she called it off, admitting that she never aspired to marriage. My father convinced her to follow through, because he had already arranged for the Imam to conduct the ceremony and all the arrangements had been made. I think for many children of the '90s, growing up in the shadow of apartheid meant being collateral for dysfunctional relationships trying their utmost to create a semblance of normality.

The constant parties at our house were manifestations of those traumas. To the unsuspecting eye, they were simply people having a good time, but they were indeed séances aimed at escaping the realm of reality. They were the summoning circles for all the demons the neighbourhood carried. An opportunity for those demons to come out and dance and laugh and sing and forget. When the realisation descended that they were still going to wake up in the same place tomorrow, violence or dronkverdriet erupted. These were the cycles many people found themselves trapped in and, for us, the cycle would continue for decades.

I had already started to understand that whatever comfort family life provided, it never stuck around for long. Being home meant always waiting to be set aside for the thrill of some foolish adult's decision. I swore if I ever had kids, I would never do that to them. I was a kid, thinking about how I could one day be a better adult. I was not very good at being a kid, that was for sure.

I had no idea that what I was going through at home made up the reality of so many children growing up in South Africa. Across spatial and class divides, we were all coming to understand the world through a similar lens and being shaped by the long arm of a past we had not experienced directly. The joy and elation playing out on our TV screens seemed to evade us in the new South Africa. Everything changed, but not a single shred of reality had altered. I often wondered why my parents' evident happiness never quite translated for me and why I seemed to pay the price for it. Everything has a price, and happiness for the wretched of the earth certainly is not exempt. I think of happiness as a trade-off for us. We rarely get to enjoy happiness without giving up something else, essential to our wholeness. Happiness is a loan, and the weaker among us often get left on the proverbial altar as a burnt offering to a god with a warped sense of humour. There is no clean break.

I should, in all honesty, have lost my faith in god here, but the fear of wrath supersedes all instincts for those raised with religion, no matter how minimally.

Making peace with dysfunction when you're still developing the sense to experience it is a hard bargain, but we rarely had choices. A choiceless existence at any level impacts harshly on your sense of self in a world that is already hostile to you.

To exist without agency in the care of people who themselves are dispossessed of it makes for such a layered manifestation of trauma, even though the circumstances we found ourselves in were privileged in comparison to many others. Material privileges without systemic power are nothing but golden handcuffs. Being dispossessed of the vocabulary to articulate trauma is the nail in a beautifully prepared coffin that lies in wait for us all in this Black journey of continued injustice.

Three

My mother stopped drinking the year I started primary school. I was completely unaware that my life had changed at the mercy of her will. I would have a loving, doting mother from that point on, and my new normal would start. She woke up one morning shortly after the New Year festivities of 1995 and stopped. Morose, with a terrible hangover, she was probably faced with the shame of what she had done the night before and, perhaps for the first time, she internalised it. The countless instances of leaving her children at the mercy of the neighbours and wasting away afternoons nursing hangovers with more alcohol started making no sense. The realisation that drinking with my father was also a trap dawned on her. This was probably the most difficult realisation to have – that her husband and life partner, on whom she was supposed to rely, was also a cruel trickster who set her up for failure. The precarity of her unequal marriage, where she was completely dependent on him for survival, was set up in such a way that she always stood to lose more than him from any bad decision.

Although they would initiate and see the parties through, when Monday came, my father would go off to work and leave my mother to her suffering. Always having taken the party to the hilt, a hangover was guaranteed in a place where moderation was a dirty word. When he came home after work and found my mother still struggling to piece herself together, he would shame and blame her for her excessive drinking.

In fact, it got to a point where he would call my grandmother to tell her how badly behaved her daughter was as a wife and mother and call for some intervention. 'Mamma, I don't know what to do with Farieda anymore. She drinks too much, and it's getting out of hand. Something has to be done,' he would say, sometimes while making sure my grandmother can hear my mother's drunken rambling in the background. In essence, he had purchased a consumable good and was not satisfied with the result, so he contacted the sellers to threaten its return for refund if they did not rectify it. This may be a very crass metaphor to relate the terms of a marriage, but these are the thought processes that often have and still do inform what heterosexual marriage arrangements mean.

In our family, there seemed to be a sadistic lust for kicking a dog when it's down, and spite often characterised these tense relations between my parents. She realised that this was a setup, since he was right there enabling and encouraging her throughout.

So, she closed the tap on everything.

Beyond her own exploits in experimenting with alcohol, my mother had a family inheritance of alcoholism to confront. She knew the shame of the life we were living very well. Her father, (Gamat) Yusuf de Villiers, terrorised his family for many years with alcoholism. My mother told me how he once smashed the windows of my uncle's car in a drunken stupor, and how he chased her down the road after she closed a window on his head in retaliation for his torturous drunken heckling. My mother was recreating the life she hated.

I later learnt that my grandfather, who was one of nine children, was also raised in an alcoholic home in District Six. His father – Abdurrahman, of whom little else is known – presumably started the cycle of shame that would haunt generations to come.

The long arm of escapism replicated trauma three times over.

Three generations long. My grandfather died as a drinker and was only slowed down by the weight of time. By the time I came to know him, he had settled into quietly sipping a few beers a week.

Whenever visiting my grandparents, who found their first stable home in Portlands, Mitchells Plain, I would be showered with high-pitched affirmations from my grandmother at the door before I ran through to greet my grandfather who was almost always in his room watching TV.

I would always say: 'Salaam, Pappa!' and he would give me a kiss, rub my head and give me anything from 5c to R2 before I ran off again. I can't recall whether he even responded to me verbally when I would greet him, but I knew I was loved.

When my mother stopped drinking, my world opened up. To know that no matter what happened, I could always count on finding the same person who was besotted with me was the new life I had fantasised about. Some days I became so attached to my mother that I locked my arms around her legs while she was cooking and wouldn't let go. She would drag me around the kitchen with a belaboured walk and never object. I think she missed me as much as I missed her and so couldn't bear to spoil my newfound excitement at being with her. I was just so happy to have a mother who planned on staying with me.

Where she went, I went, and we did everything together. I could not get enough of saying her name – Mommy. I had to say it as much as possible just to enjoy the knowledge that she would always respond. I guess a part of me had also hoped to make up for all the times she couldn't hear me calling her name, even though she was right there, within arm's reach. I was grateful to my mother for choosing me. This gratitude would form the foundation on which our enmeshment was built, because we became all we had. We would become a unit, tethered at the navel. I had a mother, and she had a companion.

The parties stopped. The home became more balanced, and my mother's attempts at creating stability for us put a damper on things for those looking for a good time. The lekker huis stopped being lekker.

My father, however, did not stop, and his drinking habits became more solitary. When Friday showed up, one could generally expect the start of his decline into a weekend of drowning his sorrows; he had many to drown. But to the outside world everything looked peachy. On the inside we were stuck between the choice of a generally sullen male figure who didn't care to speak more than five words at a time and a taunting, drunken heckler, hellbent on making us question what we did to deserve such torture. god was never in the room.

When the weekend came around, my mother would make sure I was entertained and distracted from the reality of my father's alcoholism.

Tayshira was a young teenager by this time who had no interest in the activities of a five-year-old. I was an annoyance to her, so she kept to herself or went to visit her friends. We would often get into fights, which really only went one way. Despite the fact that she probably couldn't stand me, I was quite enamoured of my sister. I wanted to be her friend and wished those fleeting moments of affection she showed me when our parents were unavailable could last. When the comfort of my imagination wore too thin to keep me entertained, I would go and see what she was doing. Barely one step into her room, she would bark, 'What do you want?!' A mousy 'nothing' would return. Trying all manner of silent infiltration, I would work my way further and further into her room, hoping she wouldn't notice. When I was comfortably in and observing her, I could not curb my curiosity and would start asking inane, annoying questions. She would entertain these at first but would eventually snap. Most times, she would have to drag me out of her room because I would fight as if I had been sentenced to eternal banishment from a medieval land. When finally locked out, feeling alone and dejected, I would run to my parents to cry foul. Without fail, I knew my mother would scold at Tayshira for being mean, and always the judgement would be, 'He's still small; he doesn't understand!' The sweet victory of vindication put a sparkle in my eye, but it was always short lived. She would get me back, and she never forgot.

On Fridays my mother would make me a favourite supper, which ranged from alphabet soup from a can to hot chips and bread. The soup was a fun, acceptable way of playing with my food. When I had chips, I would stack them on a slice of buttered bread and fold it over. I'd do this with each slice until the chips were done. Sometimes I left a few, to eat on their own. When I was done eating, she would put me on the couch with my favourite movie and watch with me while my father would get progressively more delinquent in his room. Several times during the movie an aggressive, 'Rieda!' would storm out of the room towards us.

When my mother didn't answer, it would become a protracted moan: 'Faaariiiieeedaaaaa', to which she would return a loud 'What?!'

It was usually nothing important, or a request for food. He always asked what was taking so long, and when he was eventually handed the food, he would often be spiteful and say he doesn't want it.

My mother endured the abuse of this power trip for most of her life with my father. It pains me to think how normal it had become, and after a while we would even laugh at it. I think people who are trapped in a cycle of trauma often have no choice but to extract humour out of their pain just to break out of the inevitable numbing that becomes their lives; just to, every now and then, feel something that is not an immobilising sense of despair so heavy that their senses stop responding to it. We often had nothing to laugh about except our pain, and those moments of laughter remain some of my happiest until today.

Saturdays were movie days. My mother made a point of taking us away from the misery of my father's drinking. Nearly every Saturday we would go to Tyger Valley Mall and watch a movie. The only one in the area, the mall was the central meeting point for most people in the Northern Suburbs. Weekends were a buzz of people doing shopping, coming to the movies, visiting the putt-putt course or the games arcade, called Wonderland.

It was all very exciting for me. I can still remember the electric atmosphere of hundreds of people whirring past each other and lit shop signage beckoning us to enter. The smell of freshly prepared food in the air was a deliberate but welcome lure. The first movie I ever saw in a cinema was *The Lion King*. I recall the pure majesty of seeing the animated characters in such exaggerated form on a screen 50 times the size of me. The drama of the darkness and blaring surround-sound speakers sucked me into the make-believe world. In that darkness I could escape the discomfort of my home life, which was always gnawing at me. I could forget to worry about when the day would come to an end and we would have to go back home, to a sombre darkness. We must have bought the video tape, because I remember watching it nearly every day at home after that. I watched it so much, I knew the entire script by heart.

Going back home was always a dread.

The drive was generally during sunset or after dark. When we arrived, the house would be so dark you could not see your hand in front of your face. My father closed all the shutters, which were capable of blocking out all light, and literally created his own night when he felt like it. The darkness he created would become a consistent feature of my home life, in many senses of the word. If anything, this is where I learnt of the different depths, shades and textures of darkness. All darkness is not equal.

The darkness separated him from us and catalysed my mother's increasing reliance on me as a companion. At the time, and for many years after, this served me very well, since she was the centre of my universe. She offered me the comfort and warmth of a stable mother and lifeline, while I filled the void left by my physically present but emotionally absent father. I became someone she could rely on to reciprocate her affections and investments. My mother took refuge in mothering me while my father retreated into his own world, where only he and his demons ruled.

We formed an alliance in response to my father's drunken rule over the household, since we both secretly knew what the other was going through. I was without a father, and she was without a husband. Most weeks, my father was either cranky as a result of a hangover or his A type personality, or he was drunk and relentless in his apparent efforts to disturb us. I had started developing the sense that I had to save my mother by devoting myself to her, and she developed an attachment to me that, I think, consoled her in the face of the tragic loss of the paradise her dream home was supposed to be.

Here started a long relationship of enmeshment between me and my mother. My love for my mother was no different to what I'm sure any other little boy has, and I was rightly attached to her. But my independence developed slower than necessary.

I was precious to her – for her own survival and mine – so she protected me, not only from my father, but from *all* forms of reality. Even then, in a community possibly much safer than it is today, she taught me to always be vigilant of anything that could take me away from her, either to a strange place or to a grave. For a Coloured mother, raising a child meant striking a balance between allowing childish innocence to flourish while instilling a sense of premature wisdom about the world. We are a people who exist and survive in spite of generational violence meted out to us through systems of domination. We co-exist with the violence we have also internalised and meted out to others. It was important for me to know my safety was not guaranteed in a world that wouldn't mourn my loss. Although being a child came with some semblance of the carefree innocence we saw in Hollywood films, we never had the luxury of oblivion in a world where violence, in some form or another, trailed us like shadows.

My mother and I would spend many years shielding each other within the warmth of our enmeshment. I had already imagined my adult life, perfectly laid out. I would go to university and study something very prestigious, probably medicine or something science related, and build an empire in no time. I was meant to inherit my father's house and live with my mother until her dying day. I also promised Aunty Mirrie a red Ferrari, but we all knew my mother came first. I was my father's only son, so it fell on me to carry on his work as a provider after he was gone. He reminded me, whenever he had drunk enough to show some emotion, that he did not have much time left on earth. Sometimes he would even mention how many more years he thought he would live. For some reason, he always felt it necessary to prepare me for his death very far in advance of it.

I did not understand it as a child, but I've since learnt that he knew that, for people like us, the world was not the oyster it is made out to be. It is a harrowing, frustrating, lonely place outside of the privilege we enjoyed at the upper end of an ethnic hierarchy. For me, I think he wished the ability to dream, even if he knew that my dreams would be shattered later. To me, he was the destroyer of dreams, because I did not yet live in the world he was preparing me for. I lived in a world where I wanted my father to be present and lucid for me. My one dream – of having a present, loving father – was shattered weekly.

As much as my mother tried to balance the dysfunction, she could not spare me the experience of a world that was not built for us. Though numb, my father was wiser in his more deliberate but subtle attempts at communicating my responsibility to learn the rhythm of a sick society he simultaneously tried to shield me from.

Through my eyes, my mother and I were in a constant battle with my father and his demons. I didn't see them as a married couple. I saw my father as the ruler and controller of our lives, which were separate to his. My mother and I were kin, united against the tyrannical rule of our captor. I sometimes felt bad about not being able to protect her the way she protected me, but I would always feel vindicated by seeing the comfort she found in our relationship.

Somehow, we always managed to escape the reality of our lives together. We did this through laughter in all its forms. Although much more aware of the world's pitfalls than a child would be, my mother had the disposition of one, which suited me. At any moment, a funny advert on television could send us spiralling into a dramatic fit of coordinated laughter. Playing games was a part of our routine; 'I Spy' was a firm favourite, and we could go at it for hours. The thing I appreciated the most was that my mother never tired of me and my need for her attention. This was perhaps because she needed mine just as much, but, unlike me, she had many worlds to live in.

At bedtime, she would read to me in my room, often from a

selected story in Enid Blyton's *The Teddy Bear's Tail*. She managed to transport me with just the animation of her voice, as she embodied all the characters for my amusement. There was the high-pitched voice of the rude little rabbit whose ears were permanently erect owing to a spell meant to teach him a lesson. The rumbling voice of a grumpy old man made my eyes widen with fear whenever it appeared, but the distress of the teddy bear who realised he didn't have a tail like the other toys in the nursery always kept me on the edge of the bed.

Bowing to the pressure of my attachment to her, she would get into bed with me and wait for me to fall asleep before going back to her bed.

Some nights I would wake up and realise she had left me. I would cry hysterically until she came back. It was not so much the feeling of being alone that drove me to tears, but a deep sense of betrayal. To me, she was not my father's wife but always my mother. I could not understand why she would have to pay him any attention. Why would she still pay attention to someone who was so mean to her? My childish logic might have been simplistic, but I'm sure she asked herself similar questions.

For women like my mother, I suspect life often requires the incessant inquiry into the contradictions of being caught between dependence and the vague possibility of distant liberation. I always wondered why she stayed, but I was yet to learn that the choices of a beautiful woman with a Standard 8 education were situated somewhere between lamenting an unfulfilling forced selflessness, with gratitude for at least being under the care of a husband, and the desperate grinding of trying to make a substandard living in a patriarchal world.

There were no easy choices, and the comforts we enjoyed were still more soothing than the limited ones of many of our contemporaries. Being a big fish in a small pond has its benefit, even if just for your self-esteem. Living in an unequal, raced society such as South Africa means accepting that in order for you to have some semblance of comfort, other people like you have to suffer. We were all suffering in some way or another.

Four

When I finished crèche, the headmistress, Mrs Miles, facilitated my acceptance into one of the white schools that had newly opened up to Black children. In 1995, schools opened free from apartheid rule. I could have gone to Watsonia Park Primary School, which was within walking distance from our house, but that was considered to be beneath us. Here the evidence of the divisions among Coloured people played out very starkly. Our part of the neighbourhood was generally occupied by professionals, and all the houses had the same number of rooms with varying designs and space allocations. We were the uppity Coloureds. The woman we bought our house from was an academic at the University of the Western Cape. She adorned the house with the best linens and curtains from Garlick's and Stuttafords. She gifted many items to my parents when she moved out. 'You can't drive a Mercedes-Benz with Volkswagen wheels,' she said. With that, she summed up the pressure Black middle-class people often feel – to create an image afforded by generational wealth they don't have. We were still to learn the consequences of this.

Apartheid spatial planning left no one behind and made sure that everybody knew their place. When driving down the main road that connected all the neighbourhoods surrounding ours, you would easily see the change of scenery, which became incrementally duller. When entering from the Brackenfell industrial area, you would pass through Northpine, where all the houses looked the same, as per the developer's plan.

Because drivers thoroughly enjoyed the smoothness of the road, when there were no potholes, they would often speed down there, which led to more and more speedbumps being added. These days you can't get through Northpine Drive in under five minutes with all the speedbumps and stop streets. If your car is modified or has a dropped suspension, you can expect to add an extra two minutes. Modified cars are a standard personality feature we've all come to enjoy in Coloured communities.

After a big bend flanked by fields, the road becomes Bernadino Drive, which signals the start of a new zone, Bernadino Heights, where we lived. The houses here had more of their own personality, each with a unique design feature and much more space. After another bend and a field, Watsonia Park started. If ever there were a practical example of how land was used to rank human lives, it would be the use of fields as buffers to keep people separated. In other places, railway lines were used in this way. Nothing about how we lived was coincidental. Everything was carefully orchestrated.

In Watsonia Park, the houses were much smaller and closer together. Small gardens spanned about three to four steps before reaching a Vibracrete wall and gate or just a wire fence. They walked onto gravel outside their gates. Trees were fewer here, and you would often see a puff of dust trailing the children as they walked. Next to them was what we called the skiem, the housing scheme where blocks of council flats were neatly lined up, like rows of corn on a plantation. As children are, the gravel never deterred them from finding joy. Games of soccer, hopscotch and reistou made space for the indomitable energy of childish excitement to fill the streets. The skiem was a cautionary tale of the bent cards history could have dealt us. A twisted sense of gratitude filled us when we would pass by, something similar to when people thank god for sparing them in an accident that killed other people. We happily fed on the violence of class oppression sold to us as a natural order of unnatural things.

There was always an unspoken rule that policed me never to wander into that part of the neighbourhood much like Mufasa kept Simba away from the Elephant Graveyard in *The Lion King*. A perfect metaphor for class separation. In our heads, apartheid reigned and manufactured all kinds of fantasies. The skiem wasn't safe, and the children there were not our class, as my mother would say. They spoke Afrikaans, and we spoke English. They were poor, and we had a nice house. We were well behaved and respectable; they were uncultured and vulgar. We were the better Coloureds, the Slamse; they were the Boesmans. We were the protégés of whiteness. They were the unfortunate descendants of the people who traded land for mirrors, and their lives were the price they paid for their foolishness. Ironically, the use of the term Slamse is a slur out of the spell book of white Christianity used against Coloured Muslims, but when used among Coloured people, it became a marker of status in contrast to those who had less proximity to whiteness. Being seen as Slamse by other Coloured people was simply a way of identifying that we were Muslims, but we thought ourselves more refined and cultured than the stereotype of the Slamse who seemed detached from secular society.

In the skiem, the hierarchy of Colouredness came sharply into focus. Though we were all in similar boats, it was very important for us to always remember how we were different to keep the clearly demarcated divisions intact. We kept our distance and hoped they never managed to move into our neighbourhood because, after all, we deserved better than to live next to the riff raff, as we saw it. What would happen to our neatly manicured gardens if they moved in? They didn't have our refined sensibilities and appreciation for aesthetics. The thought was too much to bear.

Ironically, there were many people in our neighbourhood who fitted the profile as those living in the skiem: Mrs Raikes and her family, for example, but her presence was circumstantial. She got lucky, we believed. Our relation to them still existed on a power differential that placed us above them in our heads. Although we appeared to be materially more propertied, we had much less security, as we would come to learn. Nevertheless, we were – at all times – the better Coloureds.

I was sent to Simonsberg Primary School to be under the care of white expertise. The decisions that were made around my education were all about proximity to whiteness and white expertise. In many ways, this also guaranteed my exposure to respectable Coloured children like me. I would be shielded from the harshness and corruption of the lower classes. The tutelage I was to receive was not only to follow a school curriculum but also a social curriculum of white civilisation. Assimilation was my secondary education.

I was one of two Coloured children in my class. The two of us instantly clung to each other – Tariq was also a Muslim boy. Although I had occupied a very privileged class position at home, I became aware of my race at school.

Everything was so white! I was enrolled to be given instruction in English, but the hegemony of Afrikaans covered every aspect of my school life.

School was the place where I learnt more about social division than anywhere. I was out of place not only for being Coloured but also for being Muslim in a predominantly white Christian schooling system. At school Islam was a stigma, but at home it was a privilege. These contradictions taught me how to play by the rules and also to manipulate them. With proximity to whiteness, I could easily assimilate and make my experience a pleasant one. When I came home, I could perform my whiteness and garner admiration from my community, though it did not always work. It seemed like a good arrangement.

I went to school and learnt suiwer Afrikaans. This idea of purity is synonymous with whiteness when it comes to Afrikaans. I've always had a very contentious relationship with the language. I was raised to believe that I come from a lineage of English speakers, although there was no evidence for this in my family history.

My mother's people on her father's side were considered Cape Malay – the 'original' people of District Six. Although some of them looked like white people, when they opened their mouths to speak, not one could maintain that illusion. They all spoke Kaaps to each other and their children.

Pappa Yusuf could hardly string a sentence together in English and was what most middle-class Coloured people would consider gham. Although this is known to be a classist slur that many of my family members would still deny, he simply was who he was. My mother always told me how abrupt and morose he was as a father and husband. My grandmother Washiela in her melancholy softness would try and start conversations about days gone by, and in his impatience, he would say: 'Siela! Moenie kô ou bene uitkakkie.' His use of idiom was not only vulgar but also creative in reimagining the metaphor of excavating memories as shitting. He was very white-passing. He had a strong jawline, almost translucently white skin and pin-straight golden-blond hair. When I came to know him, he did not have a single tooth in his mouth and refused to wear dentures. I would always marvel at how he ate nearly everything with those gums, although my grandmother made sure to cook his food to just before the point of liquification.

Mamma, originally a Christian hailing from Kimberley named Rachel Peters, spoke more English but also showed no evidence of being English speaking, since she only spoke Kaaps to my grandfather and to her siblings. There were times, I've been told, when she would use Afrikaans to fool the bus conductors during apartheid. To transform into her alter ego, Rachel de Villiers, she would dye her hair platinum blonde with peroxide. Combined with her fair skin, her blonde hair allowed her to ride the white section of the bus undetected. Funny as it may be now, the violence of not being enough remains deeply embedded in our memories of being and language. She did, however, speak English to her children, which may have been the genesis of English as a first language in our family.

Many Coloured people held the belief that English was the language of opportunity and prosperity, and proficiency in it meant self-preservation. In many ways, they were correct, and this is understandable in a capitalist society, but it fed into a conscious effort to abandon expression in their mother tongue and fed into the internalised shame of speaking a slave language. They were preparing their children for life in a white supremacist world.

My grandfather on my father's side was the conduit for a linguistic tragedy in our family. An Indian man, by apartheid classification systems, he spoke fluent Urdu. He was quite dark skinned, with thick, wavy black hair. The only recollection I have of him as a young man is set in pictures, since he was quite old by the time I was born and was already balding. As many did, he had himself reclassified as a Cape Malay, and in an attempt to avoid sabotage of his efforts, he forbade the speaking of Urdu in the home. We lost a language and a heritage in the blink of an eye. By design, he also then spoke predominantly Kaaps to my grandmother, who was also raised a Christian, and people in his immediate environments. Though I have mourned the loss of linguistic diversity in our family, the turn away from Indian culture saved my father from forced marriage to his cousin at the age of 17. He still had to run away from it, but at least my grandfather didn't try and stop him. Maybe losing Urdu was a small price to pay in the end.

My parents also spoke mostly Kaaps to each other, which is where I learnt to speak it too. At home and in the community that was often our language, but at school it became a shameful, bastard tongue. A deviant tongue needing correction.

The shame I was quickly becoming acquainted with threatened to sabotage my daily efforts at assimilation, so I had to split myself. I performed whiteness at school and enjoyed a privileged Colouredness at home. The tightrope one has to walk to relate to two worlds while making sure they don't bleed into each other is petrifying, even for the most seasoned daredevil. You never know when you've overstepped until it's too late and you've already been reprimanded. It is ironic that my parents consciously sent me to white schools and performed palatability for the white gaze, but at the same time reserved resentment for white people who still treated them like intruders in their own land. I am grateful for it all, if only for the fact that it reminded me that no matter how well I assimilate, I will never be white. This was a crucial realisation in teaching me not to abandon who I was.

Being a Muslim also provided a certain level of privilege at home, unlike at school. Aside from our family proximity to whiteness, Islam was often considered much stricter than Christianity. Muslims were considered much less modern in their practice of spirituality, which in reality was a misreading of Christian dominance in our society. Islam only seemed less worldly because social interactions did not centre on the acceptance of Islam as a default practice. In a community like ours, which was not predominantly Muslim, seeing people practise their faith daily – through calling each other to prayer five times a day, wearing Islamic clothing, fasting from dawn until dusk, and generally avoiding non-Islamic practices – created the expectation that we would have a super spirituality. Practising Islam often meant being in conflict with the western lifestyles that most people aspired to and indulged in as far as their finances could carry them. Being a Muslim meant no mistakes, no concessions and no diversions.

Navigating these expectations in my community placed a heavy burden on me. At school I had no religion, because if you were not a Christian, your religion did not exist. At home it was assumed that we all practised our rituals on the clock and that our lives were consumed by them.

The shame of practising an imperfect Islam, with the perceived anomaly of having an alcoholic father, weighed heavily on me, from both the other Muslims and Christians. Society finds multiple ways to police marginal bodies. Being co-opted into these systems from birth, you would assume I wouldn't know the difference, but I was always keenly aware that there must be a different way. In me was always the intuition to discern the mechanics of oppressive systems, wherever they manifested themselves. I didn't have many choices then, but I knew my day would come, and when I gained autonomy, the life I was given would not remain the life I choose.

It would be a long time before I got to fully choose, but the years leading up to my decision to choose a different life were filled with anxiety, questioning and failure. I would face years of judgement for not being a quintessential Muslim. Yearning for a balance somewhere between the modern western world and fulfilling my obligations to my creator through a system at odds with the rhythm of daylight hours, I always found my faith to be a chore, because it just could not be reconciled with everyday life of 1990s South Africa. Everything I did required double time, and maybe this was because I found myself outside of a community that practised Islam as a primary lifestyle – a way of life, as they called it. Even within the privilege, the otherness was simply exhausting to bear. I would still have to face many more contradictions and obstacles when my sexuality became pertinent and I became mukhalaf, of the age when I was expected to carry full responsibility for my religious practices. The more I understood about what was expected of me, the less it made sense.

I wished for life to be simpler, and I could never understand why we had to be so constrained by rules we couldn't explain. What could possibly be so wrong in merely living life, with kindness and thoughtfulness, neither bowing to anything nor towering over anyone? I was always lost in religion, where I was to be grateful that I was chosen for salvation from eternal damnation. Where I was preparing, through an internalised superiority, to receive my reward in the afterlife. How was I to reconcile this with the knowledge that my friends and neighbours were not following me into paradise, and how could I bargain for their entry to join me? It all seemed far too anxiety provoking for me, and if I had my way, I would just live free of worrying about a world I was yet to see.

Religion is politics dressed up in the divine. It truly is one of the smartest cons of history, to take the construction of the human condition and retell it through a fantasy that validates what is wrong with the world. The power of men, white people, heterosexuals, cisgendered people, abled-bodied people and even rich people is all normalised through the scripture, creating the illusion that they precede the human condition when, in fact, they are inspired by it. The self-fulfilling prophecy has prevailed for centuries and remains the best example of how the world is the making of the smartest orators.

Living life as a religious delinquent introduced me to the messy matrix of privilege and oppression. My parents made me go to Madrasah every night of the week, yet the dysfunction in our home was the antithesis of everything being taught there. The confusion of trying to reconcile these two lives was a burden too heavy for a child. The shame of this double life was a harrowing experience; hoping that no one would find out was my daily mode of existence. When I went to school in the day and had to identify myself within the normative family structures my classmates spoke of, I felt out of place. When I went to Madrasah at night and had to relate to the unforgiving permanence of Islam as a way of life, I felt out of place – and also under surveillance. I was afraid that people would find out that I was not who I pretended to be and that my father was not who they thought he was. In my mind, we would be exposed and expelled for the hypocrites we were.

Life for a young child is scary enough with all the dangers created by adults; to live with the impending fear of disgrace adds an unnecessary insult. In a world where I already felt responsible for my mother's happiness, balancing this act started a growing resentment in me. A resentment not only for the failure of my parents to give me a normative home life, but also to the establishment that forced us to hide ourselves and attached this shame to us. I knew nothing else, but I wished it could be different.

Five

There was nothing more liberating than the feeling of walking out of school. As I left the gates, I would look around for my mother, who was always parked in the same spot, a few metres away from the pedestrian crossing managed by the scholar patrol. There were times when I didn't see her, but she had taught me never to panic. Before I started school, she drilled it into me that I had to wait for her. 'Don't walk off or go with anyone else. If they tell you I sent them to pick you up, run back into the school. I will always come to fetch you, even if I am late, I am coming!' she would say. Those days we didn't have any cell phones to communicate, so we made arrangements beforehand. She was rarely ever late.

When I got home from school, I would usually change into play clothes while my mother made me something to eat. I was much more privileged than many of my schoolmates whose mothers had to work and so would stay at aftercare until late. After lunch, I would watch cartoons on TV. We didn't have much homework in those days. Later, I would go and look for a friend, so we could play in the street. I would always end up playing with Nessie, who was my best friend at the time. I always felt more comfortable and understood with girls. They never questioned why I wasn't like the other boys, and they didn't play games that were too rough and strenuous. I loved playing huisie-huisie, which involved us emulating our parents in a game of making a home using dolls as substitutes for ourselves. There was also a variation, called skooltjie-skooltjie, that emulated school life. I still wonder why we had to repeat the word to denote the game version. At other times we played more physical games – such as skiptou, reistou, skalooloo, brandtens, nikkis, wegkruipentjie and others – which would give us a thorough workout. The game would just be getting to the best part when the sun started setting.

'Jamil, come now!' My mother's voice came rushing up the road as sunset approached. Maghrib, the Islamic sunset prayer, was approaching, and that meant I had to get ready for Madrasah. It always managed to put a damper on my mood because it always came at the peak of the fun. With bowed head, feeling very sorry for myself, I walked home as slowly as I could. After bathing and putting on my top and koefiyah, a very dread-filled me and Tayshira were taken to the masiet.

The mosque was a very unusual place for me, even though it was the only place of worship I knew as mine. Through the anecdotes, images and visits to churches, which were normalised in my imagination as a primary representation of a place of worship, our mosque was made strange. Again, it was something that interrupted my world view. It wasn't as ornate and artistic as the famous mosques in Saudi Arabia or Morocco, which I knew from photographs. It was a face-brick square with a white minaret and remained under construction as long as I attended. Next to the mosque was a concrete foundation of what would be an extension, but it never seemed to get any further than that and remained unattended. With its amber-stained glass panels shaped like the sun's rays, the mosque's wooden double door faced Moulana's house on the premises.

We removed our shoes at the entrance – they are not allowed inside the mosque – and stored them in a shoe rack. Then it was off to the ablution area, where we would perform wudu, or abdas, as we called it. This fulfilled another requirement for performing prayer and touching the Qur'an. Though I hardly performed abdas at the mosque because I bathed at home, the procedure dictates that one cleans the mouth, nose, face, ears, neck, arms up to the elbows and feet up to the ankles with water before touching the scripture. The ablution area also had toilets and a shower that I'd never seen anyone use.

When entering into the prayer area, nothing much grabbed the eye. The floor was covered with a thick, velvety azure carpet that stretched from wall to wall. A repetitive pattern of hollow minaret silhouettes detailed the carpet. To the left we would congregate for our nightly Islamic lesson. We would be arranged in rows on the floor, with calf-high desks to place our Suraats or Qur'ans on. Any holy book in Islam may not touch the ground and should always be elevated. Straight ahead was the mimba, from where sermons were conducted on Fridays, and to the left was a room made with drywalling where the women and girls prayed. Men and women who are not related are not allowed to be in contact during prayer because this breaks the abdas. There are contestations around this, dictated by whether the touching is done with desire or not, but I remember contact was always simply avoided. I was always terribly uncomfortable around boys and men in general, and even more so in the mosque. I knew boys only to be rough and mean, and the men these boys would surely become to be abusive and dictatorial. They frightened me.

Fortunately, I was allowed to make salaah with the girls. It was the sweetest victory for me not to spend more time than absolutely necessary with the boys. It was more than that too. Tayshira was always such a source of protection for me. Though I was mostly an annoyance to her at home, she was fiercely protective of me in public. She would fawn over me and stay ready to fight anyone who harmed me. It truly was the archetypal sibling rivalry – oil and water in private; mother hen and her clutch in public. I'm not sure that any of the other boys wanted to join the girls, but I was clearly favoured. Tayshira and I were treated differently to the other children. During lessons, one by one, we would be called to Moulana's wooden book stand with its leather thongs supporting the book. We would then recite the lines we had been given to prepare the previous night.

Any child who made a mistake would be tapped on the knuckles with a pencil, but for us he had all the patience in the world. It really helped, since I had no idea what the Arabic I was reciting meant. I always found it absurd that I was not simultaneously being taught language and comprehension, alongside the recital. Then again, cults don't explain themselves, but establish their existence as common sense in the minds of their followers.

The second part of the lesson was Fiq, a lesson on Islamic scripture and history. This was more up my alley with all its anecdotes and instruction on how to actually practise this religion I was learning in a foreign language. This was the more relaxed part of the evening… until we had to be quizzed. But again, Tayshira and I were spared the humiliation of punishment. In later years, sometimes my mother would hoot outside while we were in the middle of Esha'a salaah, and Moulana would signal that we were free to go.

I don't remember ever leaving Madrasah feeling spiritually fed or enlightened. All I felt was relief for being set free to return to my everyday life. On other occasions I visited the mosque on Eid mornings with my father, who on that day would be so warmly received and welcomed by the congregation we referred to as the Jamaa. It always baffled me, since my father did not practise a single semblance of Islam. This was also an uncomfortable experience, because, unlike while making salaah at Madrasah, when I went with my father I did not have the safety of my sister. I had to stand on my own, in full view of everyone. I had never been taught the prayers one says between each prayer position so I would move my lips and pretend to be saying something, while watching those around me and copying their movements. I also wasn't taught the order of the different rituals and so was always in danger of doing it wrong. I was afraid of not knowing, because everyone else seemed to know what to do and how to do it. I had no way of knowing, because I was never taught. No praying happened in our home. My mother did not know how and, although he knew, my father never practised it. I felt the weight of the shame, yet again.

My confusion about my father's unlikely camaraderie with the Jamaa would be cleared up one night when my mother was yet again subjected to his torturous drunkenness. As usual, he was calling her incessantly for one or another insignificant request. The one minute food, the next minute a heartburn remedy. Sometimes he would call her to confirm that she was still there. This would usually go on for hours, but that night, there was an unexpected knock on the door. I hated having visitors. The atmosphere of our home was uncomfortable for us under those circumstances, and I would rather endure it alone than have to perform hospitality for people in an attempt to explain the dysfunction away. More disheartening was the thought of how they would judge us for living so far outside the lines of respectability. Although I knew that many of our neighbours had similar lives, theirs just seemed more functional and social. In fact, I marvelled at how neighbours like the Carelse family still turned drinking into a social event and still had fun. They had the occasional drunken argument, but that was normal to us. For us, there was no fun. Later, when I got older, I would come to learn alcohol also caused them pain, but when I looked out of my bedroom window to see them dance and laugh, all I could see was the fun we never got to have.

The tension was palpable as my mother went to open the door. It was Moulana. One night while picking me up from Madrasah, my mother had spoken to Moulana about my father's excessive drinking and asked him to make a house call to speak to him. She had hoped that appealing to my father's Muslim conscience would make him buckle under the judgement of the mosque and god, since our cries did not move him in the least. Seeing Moulana, I immediately felt a warm rush of blood punctuate my face. I was not at all prepared to perform the pious Muslim role, and the house told a better story than I ever could.

'Asalaamualaikum, Antie Farieda,' he said as he entered the house. 'Is Boeta Farouk here?'

I looked at my mother, and she stared back at me, almost as if to say, 'Can you believe this shit?' What was the point of trying to talk to a drunk man about his drinking behaviour?

'Farouk, Moulana is here for you.'

An audible scrambling came from the room as my father tried

to compose himself while my mother placated Moulana with small talk. I'm sure she offered him something to eat and drink, but I was not focusing on anything but my swirling thoughts propelled by the embarrassment I imagine had started precipitating on my skin.

Although the lights were on, the house was even darker than the dark night outside. It smelt like cigarettes and food. The rakams on the wall hung slightly skew in anticipation of the bullshit that was about to play out. They were wiser than me.

Although I was embarrassed, I was naively hopeful that the shame of having Moulana witness him in that state would inspire my father to change. I was yet to learn just how deeply invested men were in affirming their god-given rights to rule over their households in all the ways that flatter the little boys in them who never got to be loved.

After a few minutes, my father emerged. He was wearing the slacks that had been lying in the corner of his room since he took them off. They were severely creased. His shoddy attempt at brushing his unwashed silver-grey bed hair, which had by now acquired permanent indents from sleeping, did little to improve his obviously drunk demeanour. Just when I thought it couldn't get any worse, he pulled out a koefiyah and put it on his head. It was, honestly, the biggest mockery I had ever seen.

'Asalaamualaikum, Boeta Farouk.' Moulana's awkward voice already failed the conversation.

'Asalaamualaikum, Moulana.'

I don't remember much of the conversation, or whether I stayed in the room. As much as I wanted it to be over, I also felt saved. Finally, someone came to our aid. At the same time, I was also afraid that Moulana would now see us differently and treat us badly when we went back to Madrasah.

The meeting ended, and Moulana was bid a hearty farewell. There were laughs and brotherly handshakes. The mood was a bit too festive for my liking. My father walked straight back to his room and continued his little séance with the spirits – liquid and otherwise. Nothing changed.

A few weeks later, my dad came to fetch me from Madrasah, as he did sometimes. He didn't wait for me outside but came into the mosque to join us for Esha'a salaah. He had never done this before. After salaah was done, all the men gathered to elect a chairperson for the mosque governing board, which was in charge of the mosque and Moulana. I found it very strange that my father would attend such a meeting, since he hardly attended to his other obligations as a Muslim. Then I thought that maybe after the talk with Moulana he had decided to be more diligent about his faith and get more actively involved in the activities of the mosque. Even that theory seemed shaky, since my father displayed no intention of taking any of Moulana's counsel to heart.

My father was elected chairman that night and, before we left, he handed over a thick envelope of money. He had successfully bought the mosque's respect, complicity and preferential treatment for his children. Though not fully cognisant of it at the time, I realised later that I had witnessed how money and its associated power manages to corrupt even the most sacred institutions. Under my father's tyranny, the mosque was one of the last resorts to seek, and he managed to circumvent that too. He was officially beyond reproach.

I slipped deeper and deeper into shame; this time being dragged down by the weight of despair. Every person I could look up to for guidance or counsel was compromised by their own greed. Though it would seem the protection from punishment could placate a child's mind, I was devastated that Moulana and all the men of the mosque, who should provide us – and mostly my father – with moral guidance, were now his employees. Nobody in that position would dream of biting the hand that feeds them. Yet another door shut in our faces. We were again on our own.

Life went on, and many more evenings of fervent play were interrupted by my mother's shrill voice calling me to get ready for Madrasah. Some nights, Moulana would bring his two-year-old son to the mosque to play while we recited our lessons. On one particular night, he brought a set of building blocks along to keep Mujahid entertained while he taught us. After we had all finished our recitals, we were given tasks to complete in silence. We sat in rows on the carpet in total silence as Moulana watched over us. I was firmly engrossed in my task when I heard him question one of the older boys, Tariq, about what he was doing while tapping him on the knuckles with a ruler. His response was unclear to me, but within seconds he was on his feet and standing chest to chest with Moulana.

'So, you want to be big man huh?'

Moulana was at least a head shorter than Tariq, flinging his authority up at him. Tariq stood silent but heaving in anger. Moulana picked up two of Mujahid's building blocks and started bashing them on either side of Tariq's head. The sound of the blocks smashing into his head echoed through the mosque.

'Come, show me how big you are! You want to be a big man, huh?'

A full assault was happening in the mosque, right before my eyes. A young boy was being beaten by a moulana in the mosque. The rest of us were too stunned to do or say anything. We were also scared, as many had already been conditioned to fear the tap of his pencil. We moved over to the side and got out of the way.

Eventually Tariq backed down and left. Everything went back to normal. Nobody ever spoke about the incident again. My entire view of the mosque and its occasional place as a sanctuary in my life started to change. I could never quite see Moulana the same again. I could never have imagined that such an angelic face could hide such cruelty. Though I did not fear for myself because I knew I was protected, I hated Madrasah even more.

I WAS ALWAYS AWARE OF my sexuality. I am not sure whether I had the language for it, but I knew I was not going to grow up to live the lives I saw around me. More importantly, I knew it was forbidden. I think I knew that before I even knew what it was. Up until that night in the mosque, I had existed in my difference. The sexuality of children is hardly ever acknowledged anyway, so the idea of naming my difference as sexuality was out of the question, even though everyone had a pretty good idea of what it meant.

That night in the mosque I witnessed how invasive the violence of toxic masculinity is. It didn't matter that the mosque was supposed to be a sacred place that existed above all the cruelty of the human condition. I realised that the mosque too is a manufacturer and enabler of toxic masculinity, because the mosque is but the product of its leaders, and Muslim men have been the gatekeepers of faulty doctrine. Whatever the cisgender, heterosexual man says is Islam, and that is how we were taught. You learnt very early on that if you did not fit that description, you would bow to the power of that man and that would then become Islam. A constraining, suffocating force protected by the fear of god. The man who is god. The god who is man.

In the mosque that night, I started developing a fear of having my sexuality uncovered. I saw myself on the outside of Muslim masculinity and quite powerless to protect myself against it. Surely, it was something to seek protection from, since it never presented itself as a nurturing force. From my grandfathers to my father, I have seen systemically disempowered men rule with tyranny. Although two of them were not overly religious, their particular brands of masculinity all reeked of the self-righteous omnipotence of Muslim sensibilities. I started to fear my truth and how it would further cement my place in the margins of Islam as an imperfect, dysfunctional Muslim. A Waterslams.

I started trying harder to regulate my body: my gestures, my walk, my voice, my mannerisms. I admitted myself to a bio-prison of self-regulation. Here my carefree childhood left. I was seven.

Moulana would also unravel more and more of his toxicity as the years went by. Rumour had it that his first wife disappeared without a trace and was never to be seen again. She escaped the marriage. There were also allegations that he had been molesting young boys at the school he taught at during the day and had subsequently been fired from. Although nothing had ever happened to me or the boys at Madrasah that I'm aware of, this raised serious alarm bells for my parents, and I stopped attending when I was around 12 years old.

During the incident with Tariq at the mosque, I again learnt that adults will turn into werewolves without warning, and there is nothing you can do to stop it. The people we are made to trust as children are often the very people you should remain heavily suspicious of. Childhood, for me, was like a game of Russian roulette. You never knew when it would stop being a game and become a fight for survival.

They say we spend our whole life recovering from our childhood, but they never mention what we are recovering from. The actions of deeply harmful adults who simply usurp the power that was used to hurt them – that is what we recover from. Some of us never do. We either learn to normalise what happened to us as means of justifying our own co-optation into oppressive systems, or we remain hurt and broken as the labels pile onto us. Only a few of us break the cycle of violence we so desperately wish away.

By this violence, my relationship with Islam, the world and god was forever altered, and I still have not recovered from the whiplash.

Six

Tayshira is seven years older than me. The gap between us was big in every other way too. Our experiences of the world were so vastly different that I kept on wondering whose bright idea it was to put two young strangers under the same roof. It would take a long time for us to find common ground on which to relate to each other. I would follow her around, and when she found me impossible to shake off, she would tell me a long story about how my parents found me in a junkyard and adopted me. No matter how many times I had heard the story, which was always the same, the conversation would always go the same way.

'I don't believe you. It isn't true,' I'd quack.

'It is. Go ask Mommy. You're not even my real brother.'

The tears began welling in my eyes as I would storm off to confirm.

'Mommy! Shira says I'm not your child. Is it true?'

'No man! She's talking nonsense! Tayshira, stop telling your brother nonsense!'

By this time, she was giggling with the satisfaction I can only imagine Satan had after collecting yet another unassuming soul. She truly was wicked at times, but it was to be expected from a teenager whose world was changing.

Tayshira was growing up, and that meant wanting to experience different things. She seemed to long to create her own identity outside of the regimentation of my father's rules, none of which she ever followed.

One summer's evening, while the sun was slowly dripping from the sky, she came to ask if she could go over to a friend's house. All her friends had decided to take their hangout to Harriet's house before it got too dark to stay outside. Teenage girls have lots to talk about, and staying out on the street after dark wasn't completely safe for young girls.

Building up the courage to ask my father for anything, especially when he was sober, took a lot of doing. Speaking to him at all took courage, because you would have to prepare yourself for a sarcastic lecture or a highly condescending inquiry into the necessity of your request, most times. Other times the answer was simply no. Tayshira had built up the courage, so there was no turning back and, besides, she really wanted to hang out with her friends.

'D-Daddy?' she started.

'Yes, what's it?'

'Please can I go to Harriet's house with my friends?'

You could tell what was coming by observing my father's face. He would purse his lips and contort his face into an expression that was both puzzlement and disdain. The answer was an emphatic, non-negotiable 'No!'

My mother tried to convince him otherwise, but his word was law. I doubt that Tayshira was even given the chance to tell her friends that she couldn't join them anymore. She was under house arrest.

She stormed to her room. She was crying helplessly while my mother tried to comfort her, but that was cold comfort. Tayshira and my mother never really connected. There was always a strange distance between them, which may have had something do with the fact that she was raised by my grandmother for the first three years of her life.

When my parents met, my mother was living in Mitchells Plain with my grandparents, and my brother, Yusuf, who was one year old at the time. She financed the house through the council for R21 per month. Until then my mother and grandparents had rented houses in Woodstock, Lansdowne, Crawford and even stayed in my great uncle's cabin for a while. This life of drifting was their reality since my grandfather was removed in the 1965 District Six demolition. My mother said it was the first time she saw her father cry.

Then Tayshira came along. My grandmother revelled in getting a second chance to parent and enjoyed actively mothering her grandchildren. When my parents got married and my mother had to leave and take Tayshira to live with my father, my grandmother put up a bit of a fight. Yusuf stayed behind with my grandparents.

Those first few years must have had a lasting impact on Tayshira, because the relationship between her and my mother has remained unsuccessful for as long as I can remember. There was no comfort my mother could provide.

Tayshira became more and more withdrawn from homelife and completely stopped trying to keep the illusion of family up. In between my father's drinking and trying to act like everything was fine, she disappeared into her own world.

She attended the Settlers High School. Despite the school policy that learners had to live within a certain kilometre radius, which we fell well outside of, my father fought to get her in there. It was very popular among suburban Coloured children in the Northern Suburbs and was a status symbol among parents. After much fussing, she was accepted. The school was in Bellville, and my father would drop her off on his way to work in Airport Industria. Every morning's ride to school must have been torture for her because my father smoked in his car and kept all the windows closed. He didn't care that we were suffocating or that we would smell like smoke by the time we reached our destination. I thought she was very happy to get to school, but time would tell a different tale.

During her Grade 9 year, the school called to find out why Tayshira was missing so much school. My father, who dropped her off every morning, was naturally very confused. He confronted her about it. It turned out that every morning after being dropped off, she would make her way to the train station down the road from the school and take a train to Woodstock, where my mother's sister, Aunty Nisha lived. She would return before school ended and come home like nothing happened. Why she was going there my parents were still to learn.

Both Tayshira and I spent many holidays with Aunty Nisha and our cousins. Sacha was Tayshira's age mate, and Keinin (named after his father, Keith) was mine. Later came Reagan, who was the odd one out for years.

Woodstock was a strange place. A total concrete jungle, very different to Bernadino Heights. From my sheltered perspective, I thought gardens were a standard feature of any home, but in Woodstock they had polished concrete stoeps. It never struck me as a place for children, since there were hardly any soft landings. Most of the semi-detached houses of Argyle Street had backyards big enough for a washing line and nothing more. The street was always lined with cars because few people had driveways. Aunty Nisha's house was a one-minute walk from the very loud and frenetic main road, so the sound of cars whirring by and hooting was as commonplace as the chirping of birds, except it continued well after sunset.

Weekends and holiday mornings at their home often started with taking a walk to the main road to buy Grand-Pa Headache Powder at Balmoral for Aunty Nisha and possibly picking up some pies and doughnuts at Something Nice bakery on the way back. Though it was an odd way of life to me, it was always fun, because I had company. I suspect Tayshira also enjoyed being there for this reason. Although Uncle Keith and Aunty Nisha's relationship was also highly dysfunctional, we felt freer in their home. Kids could be kids, even though we were shouted at every second minute for making a mess – or simply existing sometimes – but we didn't take it very seriously. I suppose I also didn't take scoldings seriously there because my father contributed largely to the upkeep of their home, so in a sense it was like my home. Before leaving her sister's house, my mother would always put money in her hand. I saw the exchange of money and concluded that although my aunt was the adult in charge of her home, I didn't need to yield much to her authority because she too was a dependent of my parents', like me. I marvel at how I managed to balance my respect for her elder status with my observations, but I did.

After my parents found out that Tayshira had been bunking school, the strangest things started happening. One weekend when my father was in Germany for business, my mother filled up the car's petrol tank on the Friday evening, and the next morning, it was empty. Tayshira had her friend Natalie over for the weekend. The mystery had everyone dumbfounded. At first nothing made sense except that thieves had drained the petrol tank. Then, upon closer inspection, my mother noticed footprints in the flowerbed under Tayshira's window and started questioning the girls about what happened.

'Did you take the car?'

'No Mommy.'

The very uninspired retort comfortably nestled itself under the chin of my mother's self-professed naivety. My mother has always maintained a child-like innocence about the capabilities of humans – something that really showed up in her relationship with my father, who was a steadfast sceptic. Though I marvelled at this for years, not understanding how she could be so committed to what I believed was unthought, my mother knew better than me what it takes to survive the cruelty of a world she was often on the losing end of. She had to believe the best of people to keep her will to co-exist with them.

When my father came home and learnt of the incident, his hackles raised immediately. He never trusted anyone – not even his children. I don't think he ever learnt to trust people again after his father divorced his mother when he was four years old. Like me, he was fiercely loyal to his mother, and although he felt betrayed on her behalf, the biggest betrayal was the requirement to call his new stepmother 'Mommy' while his own mother was still very much alive. He didn't speak about it often, but every now and then, when the whisky would soak in too deep, it would come gushing out. He never stopped trying to prove to his father that he was enough. He also never stopped resenting his father for forcing him to kill his mother's living memory while handing his cheek to a stranger. An immense unforgiveness turned to perpetual scepticism governed my father's miserable lingering in the world. None of us escaped it. He let the incident with the car slide the first time.

A week later, my father woke up to find the car, which always stood in the driveway, missing. In disbelief, he wiped his eyes to make sure he was not hallucinating.

'Farieda! Kô kyk hie! Die kar is weg!'

'Wat meen jy die kar is weg?'

Almost as if to prove the impossibility of what my father was telling her, my mother indeed got up to see whether the car was actually gone. I woke up to talking outside my window. I would often sleep through the sound of my father's booming voice fuelled by the excitement that morning people usually force on the rest of us. Half asleep, half attentive, I could hear that something was wrong. I got up to find out what all the fuss was about and found my parents, Tayshira and the police outside. My sister was there to help them think through what could have happened to the car. Almost like an oracle, she suggested that they search the immediate surroundings, which seemed like a good idea. Everyone agreed.

Within five minutes, the car was found, parked in the next street. Relief and disbelief washed over everyone's faces. My father, perpetually suspicious, raised an eyebrow at my sister. He was not in the least convinced of this fateful coincidence of mercy that rained down from above. With no evidence or whisky-induced bravado to back up his theory of foul play, he placated the situation with pretence. His hackles remained raised. His redemption was fast approaching, the rest of us none the wiser.

A few weeks passed without any commotion beyond the usual fuckery of the weekly dysfunction. The car stayed where it belonged. We followed suit. My father's suspicion of recent events grew thicker and thicker.

'Ek sê vi' jou, die kind is biesag met kak in die huis.'

My mother, ever the bright-eyed optimist, was not persuaded by his prophesies of doom. It must be said that, as I grow older,

I realise the very practical value of my mother's naivety. She had her life mostly settled in the palms of other people, often strangers. The precarity of a life devoid of autonomy, removed by a system of dehumanisation that operated as legislation and tradition, is an anxiety unmatched. The agency she had was spent on extracting little comforts for herself and her children to make the world's ugly face seem a bit less scary. On the other hand, it was difficult to believe my father most times, because his suspicions were pitched at the level of premonition – a difficult thing to understand with earthly sensibilities. He didn't have earthly sensibilities. My father saw through all the lies and the threats in people, with razor sharp disdain. He defied social conventions of appropriateness and politeness, and for that he was loved and hated in equal measure. To me, it was the most unbearable thing, because it seemed that there was nobody my father came across who he didn't manage to offend. Today I wonder if he was really that horrible a person, or if dishonest people are so abundant that he was forced into a steady sceptical mistrust. I inherited some of my father's sensibilities, as I'm not in the least inclined to appease social conventions and traditions. The difference between us is that I have learnt to pretend better than he did, and so I manage to create the illusion of concern for it all, when blunt honesty is not worth spending on unwilling ears.

One Sunday morning, my father happened to be sober enough to beat the sun in rising. He had heard a sound outside. Probably prompted by insomnia and suspicion, he lifted the bedroom shutters to check on the car. It was there as it had been every day for a while, but something was amiss. He heard a ticking noise coming from the car – like it had just been driven and was still cooling down. He also noticed that the car was bone dry, with not a single dew droplet in sight. My father was no fool.

I was not aware that any of this was playing out in the driveway. By the time I woke up, nothing much was going on. My mother told me afterwards that he quietly came to investigate. As he approached, he checked whether there was anybody near the car, possibly hiding. He saw nothing. I'm sure he was already prepared for what he would find. He had suspected it all along. He may have been a drunk, but it was quite a feat to fool Farouk Khan, and if you thought you did, he was probably the one fooling you.

If the pebbled stepping stones that created a pathway from the stoep to the driveway could talk, they would probably tell of the moral dilemma they were in to either carry the weight of my father's angry steps to the car or to sink into the ground and take him with them to save my sister, who was in the car. When my father got to the window, there she was, spread across the passenger seat, hiding her head and her fear. The auto poltergeist had been exposed after months of terrorising the residents of 4 Broadway Crescent.

My father calmly opened the door. His response to major events was always confusingly paradoxical. He could scream and moan for hours about something as banal as dropping a bottle of chutney on the floor but displayed the restraint of a monk when dealing with serious issues.

These events started brewing a storm of misery that would continue for the next three years.

Tayshira refused to be confined by my father's unfair rules, which threatened to wipe out her entire adolescence. If he had his way, she would never be exposed to the outside world. He knew, like most men do, that men are trash, and keeping her confined to the house was the best way to make sure she never found out. She had nobody to relate to. Teenagers don't generally relate well to their parents, especially when one is always mindlessly drunk and the other is wallowing in the misery of the experience. Tayshira was alone, so she went looking for life in my father's car. It really was the best retort to her confinement, physically and symbolically. The danger of it all was yet to be revealed to her.

My father interrogated her about where she was going and what she was doing. She went mute. She wouldn't speak to anyone or answer any questions. What my parents were still to find out was that she got herself embroiled in a relationship with a gangster. A member of a gang specialising in robberies and theft. My parents were many things under the banner of dysfunction, but they were not intimately acquainted with criminality. In fact, we were the kind of people and Muslims who saw ourselves as superior to the Slamse

– who, as my father put it, were only good for 'lieg, brêk en steel'. This was a reference to Muslims who were mostly Cape Malay and sometimes Indian, who lived such insular Islamic lives that they hardly participated in mainstream life. They also happened to be wealthiest in the Coloured neighbourhoods, creating an illusion of middle-classness within these communities. It was an illusion, because their wealth was often a result of bending the rules of the system – or outright criminal activity. If they were not running the syndicate, they were overseeing it. Drugs, human trafficking, fraud, contraband goods, tax evasion, mineral smuggling were all covered up by a veneer of saliegheid, the kind of salvation you were assured of as long as you went to mosque, fasted during Ramadan and covered yourself appropriately. Everyone seemed to be in on the scam and, like the comradeship we see in our political arena, they all appeared to protect each other. Ironically, through everyone else's eyes, we were all the same. But we looked down on them for being criminally inclined, and they looked down on us for being Waterslamse. Naturally, the fear that would dawn on my parents at the realisation that my sister was not only dating a gangster but also a Slams was colossal.

My father's drinking got worse. He would often get himself knackered and start troubling Tayshira. He had a very deliberate way of making sure he was drunk enough to be considered out of control but still lucid enough to direct his own intentions. His intentions were to harass her, partly to understand her behaviour, which felt like a pointed campaign to embarrass us, and partly to remind her of his power. I remember one night when the harassment started, I gravitated towards my mother, as I always did when I felt unsafe. My father was in the next room, asking Tayshira questions about why she was doing what she was doing. I could hear her non-response gradually angering him, and his already booming voice became louder and louder. I could tell my mother was ready to intervene as her attention shifted from me to what was happening there. My heart rate was steadily increasing with the ominous tension that always threatened to overrun the atmosphere in the house. There was a loud banging sound coming from the room.

Tayshira was crying.

My mother walked in, and I could hear her screaming: 'No Farouk! Stop it! No! No! No!' I ran after her and entered the room as she lunged forward to wrestle the Telkom handset out of my father's hand. He was repeatedly banging it over Tayshira's head.

He retreated to his room. Despite my mother's best efforts, Tayshira was inconsolable. I don't think it was because she was distraught but rather because she had never had much of an affinity for our mother. Theirs was always an uncomfortable relationship burdened by a weird disconnect. It was as if she needed a mother but didn't want mothering – at least not from our mother. It is a disconnect that has endured. It is something incorrigible, misunderstood and unbearable. Sadness and despair made its presence known in the house like an unwelcome guest, blithely unaware of the inconvenience they cause and not particularly interested either. We went through the motions of life and somewhere, every now and then, a semblance of family life appeared. It was an on-again-off-again relationship with normalcy. I had developed an understanding, early in life, that it mattered not what your life was, but how it looked to others. We were governed by the rules of 'Wat sallie mense sê?', also known as the abantu bazothini syndrome. It would become one of the most critical social conventions I would have to defy when I finally claimed my own right to existence. Before then, for years, I laboured under the paranoia of worrying what people thought of me and my family. The paranoia would get worse.

ONE MORNING, I WOKE UP to screaming again. It was my father's voice, but he wasn't scolding someone this time. He was hysterical. He was also dead sober. I had an almost inherent skill for detecting my father's sobriety, or lack thereof. Even after two drinks, I could tell he was no longer completely sober.

Something terrible had happened. I got out of bed with trepidation. I wanted to know what was going on, but I also wanted to stay in bed and spare myself the trauma of yet another tragedy. My father was pacing up and down the living room. I noticed that

Tayshira was not in her room and, for a second, I assumed she might have been in the living room where all the commotion was. She was after all the centre of commotion at the time. But I didn't see her in the living room. I only saw the look of distress on my parents' faces.

My sister was gone. She had disappeared from her bed without a trace. Abductions were always a real thing growing up, although we managed to observe the idea from an uncomfortably mythical distance. As parents do, mine were worried about her safety, because no matter how our father terrorised us in the home, we were still his beloved children. This is often the white elephant in the room when it comes to love. We reserve the terror of our humanity for the ones we love the most, defending them against all manner of external terror. Poets and philosophers have characterised love as a euphoric puff of perfection swaddling those of us lucky enough to be chosen – but love often is terror. Perfect love is for babies who have not yet been taught how to be human. Adults labour to achieve euphoria. The terror of humanity empties love of all its romantic connotations, and over time we find ourselves more attached to the familiarity of the terror than the euphoria of love.

Word came from Woodstock that she had run away to stay with Aunty Nisha. My parents were relieved but horrified. She was only 15 and had audaciously taken her fate into her own hands. The idea that a child could decide for herself while still under the care of her parents was unheard of. The agency of children to choose a better life for themselves, no matter how badly they are treated by their parents, is a myth. In a country where too many children are abandoned by reluctant parents or orphaned by terminal illness, those of us who got to be dragged behind the physical presence of two parents are expected to be grateful. Dragging was exactly what my parents did time and time again, also as they went to fetch Tayshira from Woodstock every time she ran away.

IN PERFECT KEEPING WITH the dysfunction our lives had always been, there were times when we did normal family things. Some weekends, my dad would drive Tayshira and her friends to matinees and pick them up again. Perhaps he felt guilty for confining her so harshly without having the emotional range to explain that he was actually protecting her. Maybe he was hoping she would be pacified enough to stay and spare us the embarrassment of being a fragmented family. Worse, the embarrassment of being a father whose child didn't obey him.

I cherished those normal family moments. For a while, the life I imagined became real, and I didn't have to live in my head anymore. For a while, my family became real.

I would sometimes go with my dad to fetch my sister. Night-time drives were always magical as a child. I remember the enchantment of the city lights whirring past me on the road while the lights that congregated around Table Mountain in the distance stood still. Night air smelt different. It was as if the absence of light made the air carry smells more heavily. The hybrid between nature, humans and petrol travelling through my nostrils always let me know that something exciting was going to happen.

MY MOTHER TOOK ME along to Aunty Nisha's once when she went to look for Tayshira, who had again run away from home. My mother took me along because my father was drunk at home, though I would probably not have wanted to stay with him, even if he were sober. It was a convoluted relationship between cruelty and love that compelled my mother to rescue her daughter from the danger of a gangster only to bring her home to an abusive, drunken father. This is the brand of fucked-up choice many Coloured women have to make every single day in a society that offers them nothing but grief. In our case, class should have been a shield, but its failure only further proves the illusion.

Somehow, we ended up on the main road in Woodstock. It was a daunting bustle of cars, taxis, people and stray dogs all trying to make it somewhere. Crossing the road at its busiest could take up to five minutes at times, and the bustling ranged from busy to busiest – it was hardly ever completely quiet. My mother got out of the car and left me inside. I saw her threatening Tayshira's boyfriend about keeping my sister there in Woodstock and refusing to let her come home.

My mother was, most of the time, someone who observed social airs and graces in service to white respectability: good table manners, not too loud, appropriate attire – classy in the literal sense of the word. When she was angry, a different person emerged. Her urge to protect inspired a rage that was quite terrifying to watch. Not once did I fear for her, but for Tayshira's boyfriend I was scared.

I never understood why my parents objected so strongly to his relationship with my sister – obviously completely unaware that he was a gangster in his 20s dating a 15-year-old. To me he was always so cool and nice. Getting him arrested was not an option for fear of the harm he could bring upon my parents and the evident police collusion. The situation was a risk to us all. In her rage, my mother didn't care about that. She just wanted to bring her daughter back home.

We returned home with my sister, who was very angry. The next morning, my father made one last attempt at understanding what was going on. Her room was painted black as per her teenage-angst-inspired request a year or two before.

'Tayshira, what do you want? Why are you doing this?' my father pleaded. He sounded genuinely exasperated.

'I want him! I just want him!'

She threw a vase of roses at my father, who managed to duck. I believed my sister was possessed. My father left the room, looked at my mother and said: 'Ek is kla met die kind. Doen wat julle wil.'

Visibly defeated, my mother went into the room to deliver the message. Both my parents had reached the point of no return with a daughter who did not want to be saved.

'Pack your stuff and get out of this house!' my mother ordered.

My sister obliged.

The sadness in everyone was palpable. Feelings of immense loss and defeat descended on us. That was the last time I would see my sister for a long time. I became an only child. I had lost the only person who showed me some tenderness when my father lost patience with teaching me how to do basic maths. His angry insults drove both of us to tears. It seems silly in retrospect, but it was such a huge gesture to me, since Tayshira also struggled with maths. There is something mesmerising about trauma bonding in the way we give each other the support we are desperately in need of. The romance in the selflessness of pouring from empty cups in a world where those with full cups will gladly keep taking is addictive.

Though eventually quietly, my parents never stopped trying to get Tayshira back home. Perhaps their most extreme attempt was when they consulted a Nigerian traditional healer named Dr Ulu. Most people we knew would not give those 'bring back a lost lover' posters a second look, but my parents could not sleep knowing their daughter was fending for herself in the care of a gangster. At this point, any belief in an Islamic god made no difference to their lives. No prayers, no worshipping. The quiet desperation my parents experienced at the hands of very unforeseen circumstances took us into a new dimension of hypocrisy. I cannot fathom how helpless people who regarded African spirituality as witchcraft must have been to walk an entire journey through it. There were steps to follow and repeat visits to be made. I remember talks of shop-bought eggs being cracked to reveal hair, paper and talismans inside. There were visits where they would be asked to remove all their clothing to have incisions made on their bodies. The significance of it all was too much for me to comprehend, but it did nothing to bring Tayshira home. They had lost not only their daughter but also their religion.

Seven

I learnt to be perceptive from an early age. They called children like me 'old souls', as if it were a compliment – but we've just seen too much too soon. Growing up in an emotionally charged environment forces you to feel things your body is not yet equipped for. Our bodies grow into our spirits as they try and make space for the overload of experiences we have already had.

Although I didn't have a significantly meaningful relationship with my sister outside of her being a lifeline to me in our parents' chaos, I felt her absence. I was too young to fully experience the emotional upheaval of a runaway sister and daughter, so all I felt was estrangement. I didn't know whether she was still my sister or if she would ever come back. I wondered if you could just opt out of family. Nobody else was like us, and that was an indication that something was wrong, but life moved along. I must have accepted that she had chosen a different life, because soon it became normal to be the only child. I was the only one in the house getting ready for school in the morning, doing homework, sleeping late on weekends, greeting visitors when they came. I felt like I was representing both of us to the outside world – trying my best to make up for the glaring absence of my sister to shield us from the questions. I could not put a foot wrong, since we had already suffered one of the most devastating family break-ups. I was the remaining piece of the puzzle – unable to complete the picture but still enough to make sure the picture is intelligible, even if my own life was completely unintelligible to me.

The house became even more gloomy. Often dark, dingy and suffocating. The smell of cigarette smoke pulled into every fabric it could find on its saunter through the house. Even after a thorough clean, the scent of anxiety and regret clung. I developed a peculiar friendship with darkness, where I was both comforted by and scared of it. This would become a blueprint for many of the relationships in my life. It would not be until my late 20s that I learnt that my relationships – romantic and platonic – did not have to be uncomfortable to be valid. I did not have to feel my way through and shrink in perpetual darkness to find belonging. Growing up in emotional disarray warped my idea of human relationships. Until I stepped back and truly looked into the people I claimed to love, human relationships were simply coincidental. They were by-products of existing. Much like family.

Time seemed to have no form or shape in our home. There was an ever-enduring haunting after Tayshira left. The spirit of despair snuck around the house in near silence, alongside my father, whose late-night drunken jaunts to the fridge reminded me that no matter how much I ignored it, our dysfunction would always find me. At any given time, I ran the risk of having my heart leap out of my chest in fright, as my father's swaying shadow appeared from some unexpected nook or from behind a lonely door. The rhythm of our daily routine was slowly thrown off balance as my father tried his best to escape reality. Drinking was not only for the weekends anymore. Wednesday marked the start his reign of psychological terror. He was in his early 50s and had a lot more stamina to commit to the relentlessness of being an obnoxious, nagging drunk. Though I try, it is still difficult to pin down the true motivation behind my father's drinking. Running from his many demons makes sense, but there also seemed to be the intention to harm. He once told my mother that he would never stop drinking because then she would have no problems. I have run this over in my mind so many times to make sense of it. What level of non-concern must one have reached to say something like this – and possibly mean it? Understanding and offering my father compassion for his indiscretions is a treacherous journey. I too have experienced my own devastation at the hands of time, facing a world that seeks to annihilate me. I have developed an empathy for my father and his attempts to escape his reality, but overlooking the very intentional harm he caused does me no justice. He will forever be a source of emotional turmoil when I behold him as a whole person, and not the pieces my memory has sliced him into. He was a hurt person, but he was also very intentional about spreading that hurt. He remains a difficult memory to hold.

In our family, we could spend years in discord, but never was writing each other off an option. Angry as we may have been at each other, we ambled along in the grips of familial ties. It is somewhat tragic and admirable at the same time to see people hold so tightly onto things that may or may not be dead. As a result of this conditioning, it was always difficult to know whether I was the one resuscitating or killing my relationships by holding on.

My parents – mostly my mother – still tried to maintain contact with Tayshira, still tried to bring her back home. My father had mostly relegated himself to an encouraging observer. When he checked out of a situation, and declared his divestment, little could bring him back into the fray. He would, however, be there when the fire burnt itself down to ash, sometimes to gloat, sometimes to offer a hand, but mostly both.

As sure as the sunrise, he did welcome her back when she finally agreed to cut ties with her boyfriend and come back home. She finished her last year of school at home, and everything seemed restored, but it was never meant to last. Tayshira always had a mind of her own and a determination to flout rules and authority, making my father's house a very short-term residence once again.

I was silently floundering at school. For a while, primary school was a struggle, except for languages and other social subjects. My academics were not the only struggle I faced. I tried desperately to get through the anguish of children's cruelty and adult judgement undetected. Being an effeminate boy in a heteropatriarchal society is one of the most horrific childhood experiences. Somehow, because I was gay and knew it, the taunts and the insults were a form of preparation for the rest of my life. While living through it, I internalised such a harrowing existence as my place in society. I understood that people like me were a betrayal to society and therefore deserved to be punished. I could see no other life ahead of me. I also felt I was a danger to anyone who interacted with me, for I would cast my voodoo on them and snatch them from normality. I came to believe that nobody, especially not other boys, were actually meant to treat me with humanity and kindness, lest they encourage my deviance or be infected by it. I wonder about the boys who were not gay but saw no value in performing their evolving gender. The sissy boys accused of being someone they are not and taught to hate boys like me for the similarities we share. My identity was – and still is – an accusation. I spent many years running from the wagging fingers and threatening eyebrows. I was always looking for shelter from the stares and the questions, spoken and unspoken. I was a silent refugee, always fleeing persecution internally while appearing to belong and pretending to enjoy it. The shame of being the wrong kind of boy locked arms with the shame of being in the wrong kind of family.

I dreamt of inviting my friends to my house. I imagined how we would play and eat delicious snacks my mom made. On hot days we could even swim. But I lived in a dungeon, with a dragon who guarded it fiercely. My father's counter-social, unpredictable drinking meant potentially exposing my friends to the dysfunction of our contained chaos, or – worse – to the insults of a deranged man looking for a sadistic fix of grandeur. There was also always the chance that he would walk into the living room in his underwear or naked while I had my friends over. The possibilities for embarrassment were quite endless, so it remained safer to keep everyone away.

I refrained from discussing my home life, like other children do when a Monday comes around, to share the family fun they had on the weekend. I rarely had similar stories to tell. All I had to say was how my mother and I had to leave home for most of the weekend to avoid sitting in the misery of my father's alternate universe. Even as a young boy, around 10 or so, I knew that what we were doing was escaping home. My mother and I had genuine fun together on our days out at the movies, or the putt-putt course, but there was always an element of pretence. We walked around with a niggling worry that something bad might be happening at home. I'm sure my mother thought about this more than I did. We, too, were trauma bonding in some ways. Try as we may have, we couldn't achieve the same mother/son euphoria we envied in the adverts and brochures. There was always something missing from, or maybe attached to, our bond. Ours was a relationship that existed in spite of our home and not because of it.

As time went by, and I grew more aware of my reflection in the mirror, my childlike apprehension for the world grew into anger. Anger is an emotion that is readily attached to Coloured people. The stereotypes about our emotional volatility, particularly the propensity for violence, is something that has burdened my people for centuries. It has robbed us of the opportunity to achieve complexity. It has made it difficult for us to own our identities and our histories. Exposing ourselves to critique, as I often do, is also hard when the risk of being reduced to an eminent stereotype is always hanging over our heads. I was afraid of my own anger and afraid to claim my right to anger. Anger was an admission of guilt to every sweeping generalisation held against me, and not the toothless kind held against powerful people aimed at highlighting their violence. It was a generalisation that had the power to constrain my life chances as happened to many of the generations who went before me.

Despite the threat of a stereotype, I was slowly seduced by my anger. I was angry at my father for refusing to give me the courtesy of the normative life everybody else seemed to enjoy. If he could not commit to that, I would have appreciated a pretence. At least, we wouldn't stand out as the incomplete family. My mother was always answering awkward questions regarding the whereabouts of my father. It is not socially correct to tell the whole truth when asked about your life, so she never told the prying eyes that he was in the throes of a yet another drunken binge. There was always a readily available lie to mimic normativity – and, after all, a man who didn't spend much time with his family wasn't an anomaly. I yearned, confused, for my father's presence. Not so much because I needed him around or even liked being around him, but to create the image of the normal family. Perhaps, knowing that he was in a nearly catatonic state at home made me exaggerate the expectations of people. I thought they secretly knew but wanted to embarrass us by asking the question. The anxiety of managing my father's public image really suffocated me. Ironically, he had no such desire and would rarely go out drunk in public, but I projected my own need for normativity onto him. I carried the shame and embarrassment he seemed to shirk.

At school, it became even more imperative to keep up appearances. Despite navigating a gauntlet at home, I started excelling at school. I decided that if I could not control my father's behaviour, I would find affirmation elsewhere, and I found it in the arts. My love for singing and drama shone through. I was in the school choir, singing solos. I joined the speech choir, I did unprepared reading, prose and poetry. I was a regular at the Tygerberg Eisteddfod and never once got anything below an honourable mention – although that was only once. My comfort zone was honours and highest honours. Every year I was called onto stage at the school prizegiving. Those were my mother's proudest moments. I remember the unbridled joy beaming from her face as she exchanged congratulations with the other parents. These are some of my most cherished memories – being able to make my parents proud. My father's glaring absence from all the celebrations was a hard pill to swallow. Again, I think the worst was the knowledge that he was not away for any legitimate reason, but to run from reality. Looking back, that was actually a very legitimate reason, but when you have children, you commit to certain responsibilities, the least of which is showing up to their prizegiving ceremonies.

I always mourned my father's absence as soon as the ceremonies ended. A combination of sadness and dread came over me as I lived through yet another missed opportunity for him to see me be excellent and prove that I am worth respect enough to grant my wishes of a normative life. The dread set in on the way home, when I would have to present my accolades to him knowing that he would be too drunk to appreciate them. I would either be met with drunken euphoria or insults for not doing well enough. Achievements had conditions to my father. If it wasn't the best, or close to it, it was not worthy of praise. I never knew what I would be walking into. Either way, he was bound to spoil my good mood.

One year, he decided to come along. Sombre, sober and probably craving a drink, he stayed visibly agitated throughout the entire ceremony. My mother's nerves were frayed. Constantly remarking about how long it was taking, he suffered through, but my mother vowed never to take him along again. He was truly a conundrum. Too miserable to relate to anyone when sober and torturously obnoxious when drunk. I kept excelling anyway.

My Grade 6 year was drawing to a close, and the new prefects for the next year were soon to be chosen. The prestige of the title was everything to us, even if the role was simply ceremonial. Prefects were the chosen ones deemed responsible and honest enough to act as secondary figures of authority – extensions of the teachers. The position was an early introduction into the power matrix of society. We all wanted a taste of the power to discipline or at least wield the idea over our peers. The rush of staying in constant favour with the teachers was addictive. Accepting the opportunity to move up in the hierarchy of importance only seemed logical. In our year, 2000, Mrs Lategan was in charge of managing the prefects. She was also my geography teacher. I was somewhat of a teacher's pet in general and did quite well in her class. She liked me for my well-mannered demeanour and obedient disposition.

Most of my teachers did, except for the hypermasculine PT teachers like Mr van Lille and Mr Louw. I hated PT for the cesspool of toxic masculinity it was. I would often forget my PT clothes, which was a cardinal sin. Mr van Lille made it his job to show us no mercy because, apparently, 10- to 11-year-old boys needed to be so harshly dealt with that they would instantly transform into the men society needed them to be. I was singled out for my sin and made to stand topless with my hands above my head. He took a wet towel and whipped my abdomen, provoking silent tears to stream down my face. I wouldn't dare make a sound, because it would encourage Mr van Lille to whip harder and longer. I had never considered myself too well acquainted with the experience of slavery until recalling this incident. My ancestors must have been wailing as they watched my turmoil. To the untrained eye, it was just a teacher disciplining his student, however harshly. To the critical eye, it was a white man whipping a slave descendant for his disobedience. I remember very vividly that this never happened to the white boys who were affirmed by his surrogate parenting towards them. These are the aggressions we refer to as children of the Rainbow Nation. That elusive rainbow drips tears and is tender to the touch in our memories. To our abusers, the rainbow served as a luxurious velvet carpet cushioning their feet as they walked all over our humanity.

At the time of the prefect nominations, I was caught talking in Mrs Lategan's class. She scolded me before the entire class. I always made sure that I avoided trouble or any negative attention, so I was devastated that I had disappointed one of my favourite teachers. In my head, she had cast me out and written me off. I would never again enjoy her praise and adoration. On the day prefect nominations were to be made, we were asked to return a letter of acknowledgement and permission signed by our parents giving the school the go-ahead to initiate us as prefects should we be chosen. I didn't even let my parents know about it, nor show them the letter. I was convinced that Mrs Lategan had already dismissed me as a viable nominee because I had disappointed her. When she saw me at the end of the day, she asked: 'Jamil, where is your letter?'

'I didn't bring it, Miss,' I responded.

'Why not?'

'I thought you were upset with me, so I couldn't become a prefect.'

'No! It doesn't work like that. Have your parents signed?'

'No, Miss. It's still at home.'

'Go to the secretary and ask her to call home and ask your mom to bring the letter and hand it to me before school ends.'

I was overjoyed. I couldn't believe I still had a chance and that I was so foolish and dramatic to think that she would count me out for something so silly. I ran to the secretary with a newfound confidence, armed with Mrs Lategan's instruction. I got on the phone, and a woozy, slurring voice answered. It was my father, drunk again.

'Daddy, where is Mommy? Can I speak to her please?'

'She's not here. She's in Woodstock.'

My heart sank to the floor. How was I supposed to get through this, with only my father to help me? I was sure he wouldn't be able to find the pants he had worn the previous day, let alone an obscure letter buried somewhere under a stack of papers on my desk. But it was my only option. I had to try and explain where the letter is and get my father to sign it and bring it to me, in 20 minutes. The odds were stacked against me. I waited at the office. Eventually he arrived, visibly intoxicated or recovering from it. His hair was half groomed due to an unsuccessful attempt to brush down the indents left by the pillow. It was an overcast day, so he wore a black-and-beige jersey with a festive pattern on the chest. His creased beige slacks were draped over his sandals. He was neat enough to come across as a functioning member of society, but when you looked at him for long enough, you could identify all the half-ass coverups he attempted before leaving the house.

I don't recall if he brought the letter, or whether it was too late by the time he arrived, but I was deeply disappointed. After all the trouble I went to with that last-ditch attempt to be a prefect, nothing paid off. All I got was bringing my slightly drunk and hungover father to school for everyone to see – my worst nightmare. All I got was public humiliation. I believe now that hardly anyone noticed or cared but, to me, every person who passed by us was fully aware of the situation and was judging us severely for the audacity to appear in public in that state. The bell rang, and that was my cue to go home without any chance of becoming a prefect. I didn't even bother explaining to Mrs Lategan what happened. I had disappointed her again and had no business stating the obvious. Another let-down courtesy of my father.

My final primary school year had arrived, and things were only getting worse. After working for Rudolf Chemicals for 13 years, my father had reached a tipping point. He was a director on paper but not in practice. He had already been in rehab twice, fully paid for by the company. His boss, the CEO of the company in Germany, had brought in a director for the Durban operation for three times the cost my father came at, including all benefits and perks due to directors. My father was earning R10 000 per month before tax. As time went by, my father started discovering this, which fuelled his drinking even more. He had a terrible habit of drunk dialling to tell people all the things he never had the courage to say when he was sober. Almost every member of his family has received a thorough tongue lashing late at night when his Dutch courage kicked in.

His boss had become the latest recipient of his wrath. To me it was just another drunken tirade playing out, and it sounded excessively aggressive because it was all in German. I would later learn that my father had learnt of his under-compensation while having to provide technical and logistical support to his colleague in Durban. He was demanding equality and fairness. His CEO found every trick in the book to justify the inequality. My father, to his detriment, had no manner of speaking under any circumstances. When he was angry, there was no cordiality. These tirades would play out over many nights, every time ending further from resolution. My father started staying home from work or going in late more often and subsequently getting drunk more often. During this time, I would find him drunk when I woke up to get ready for school and in the same state when I came home. Some days, he would let the entire day pass him by while we continued as usual.

It also came to light that a mismanagement scandal was about to be exposed. In the textile industry, there were dirty games when it came to competition. In order to make sure that Rudolf was the top-selling company, my father paid backhands to the dyehouse managers for their loyalty. This was an informal instruction that came from Germany. Now the company was about to be investigated for this bribery, and all the paper trails led to my father. When the time came, the investigation would surely find that my father acted alone, because nobody else would have admitted to their involvement. He was faced with the choice to be fired or resign. In what would be the last conversation with his CEO, he drove the final nail into the coffin when he called him 'a fucking Nazi'. My father resigned and negotiated to buy the company car for R25 000.

My last prizegiving at primary school saw me walk away with certificates and trophies. I was chosen to accept the trophy for outstanding performance on behalf of the senior speech choir. I was vindicated after missing the chance to be prefect. Again, my joy was dampened by the misery at home, which had now reached the most epic proportions. Aunty Mirrie attended with my mother. I was grateful that she came to witness my achievements, but it could not soothe my deep regret and longing for a typical family that everyone could recognise.

Yet I was still at my most hopeful at this stage. I just could not give up on the possibility that, one day, I would be good enough for my father to choose me over alcohol. No matter how many times he disappointed me, I always believed that I was not doing enough to convince him that I am worthy of his attention and affection. My yearning itself was a contradiction, since I had a deep fear of my father for his abrasive and abusive ways, but I had constructed a fantasy based on how I saw families represented in the world. On the one hand, I wanted a father who was present and engaged, while on the other, I was as afraid of him as I was of men in general. A relationship with my father was unattainable – and that remained a comfort and curse to the end of his life.

PART II
SINKING

Eight

There was no backup plan for us after my father was forced to resign. Although our lives didn't change much – my father's pride would not accept defeat – we were trying to plug a hole in a dam that was bound to break. During my father's time at Rudolf Chemicals, we lived a really good life, despite him not having much cash. He was given an expense account to entertain clients, which was a part of the bribery. Every festive season, he would go out and buy boxes and cases of alcohol as gifts for his clients as well as gifts for their wives or girlfriends. Often, he would drink half of it before it was time to hand it out and had to replace it. My mother and I always laughed at this. Since the spending on the account was largely unmonitored, we would often enjoy dinners and other kinds of entertainment at the company's expense. Restaurants, theatres and hotels were all at our disposal, and we lived a simulation of rich white people's lives. Every year, we booked a generous holiday at the Van Riebeeck Hotel in Gordon's Bay. We went there so often, I ended up befriending the receptionist, Eloise, who built a camaraderie with my father over her ability to speak German too. We became so well acquainted with Eloise that she invited me to her family home in Pniel, between Stellenbosch and Franshoek one year for Sunday lunch. Coloured people certainly know how to prepare a table, so accepting the invitation was a no brainer.

My father acted like he owned the Van Riebeeck, always loud and familiar with all the staff. We also got to know the owner, Mrs Wilhelmina Fenton – a rich Dutch heiress who had bought the hotel as a retirement investment. She was a sweet old woman who also took a liking to me and treated me like a guest in her own home. The hotel was eventually closed and demolished after Mrs Fenton's much younger English husband defrauded her of nearly all her millions and took off. She had to sell her assets to regain some kind of liquidity. I felt bad for her, and I was even more mortified that our beloved hotel was no more. Where else would we be able to live out our fantasies of being rich white people?

When the privilege of the expense account was taken away, revolving credit stepped in. My father was not simply proud but arrogant about the image he had created through the illusion of wealth. His entire being depended on his image as a rich and powerful man, especially in relation to our neighbours. He was perceived to be the richest man in the neighbourhood – or at least the flashiest. This is why he was willing to humble himself to negotiate to keep the company car, although it was on my mother's insistence that he fight for it. From her perspective, she could not embarrass us, her children, by letting the Mercedes-Benz disappear from the driveway. Neighbourhoods as classed as ours were a self-imposed prison of working shame. Nobody wanted the next person to know that they have regressed or downgraded for any reason. The pressure to remain upwardly mobile and to continue accumulating more kept everyone on their toes. We were, after all, the better Coloureds who lived in the nice house, so we could not drop the ball. Sliding back was far more devastating than committing oneself to perpetual struggle and worry behind the façade of upward mobility. For our family there was even more pressure to maintain our status, because we were the best of better Coloureds. Holding onto the top spot in the hierarchy was an endeavour worth every risk.

Revolving credit meant that my father could keep us in the lifestyle we were used to, although slightly less extravagant, but he was racking up a hefty bill he had no idea how to repay. Our home loan agreement was what was called an access bond. It had a credit facility attached to it which allowed him access to money that was offset against the remaining balance on the home loan. How this seemed like a good idea to any reasonable person escapes me, but when considering the vice grip that a patriarchal man's ego has over him, I can see how the thought of admitting his inability to keep providing was tantamount to death. To us, it was all legitimate money, because my father allowed nobody into his finances. He was in charge, and that was the end of the story.

Luckily, because of his expertise and connections in the textile world, my father found the perfect opportunity to work mostly from home. It was basically the same job, but it was commission based and had no benefits. His ability to sell stood him in good stead, with the loyalty of all the dyehouse managers who supported him in his fall from grace. They were ready to follow him wherever he went. His income was uncapped and determined by his own tenacity to sell textile auxiliaries, ending his brief encounter with humility swiftly. He earned good money for the next few years, but at no point did financial wisdom kick in. Our lives were to be kept as aesthetic as possible to appease the people's eyes.

We were always living above our means. After the renovations in 1994, there were constant upgrades being done to the house that were not necessary. Initially the house was carpeted, then parquet floors were installed in the passage, then they were replaced by tiles, which we settled on. The window adornments changed with my mother's mood. First vertical blinds, then Venetian blinds, then finally vertical blinds again, which were changed every time the walls were painted a different colour. We were probably Verimark's most loyal customers – we owned almost every invention they ever made. I still have a scar on my finger, which has forever altered my fingerprint, where I sliced a piece off while wiping the Twista blades. The Twista resembles a butter churner, but instead of whisks at the end, it has severely sharp tiered blades that chopped vegetables up in no time. I think it was my mother's way of getting her money's worth for having to endure my father's endless psychological terror.

She had no access to or control of the money she witnessed being spent around her, so compulsive shopping for things besides the usual necessities may have been her way of getting some enjoyment out of it. My parents created a reckless spending culture and a generally irresponsible relationship with money. Worse, money that we didn't have or could not comfortably repay.

Since my father was not visibly a part of the mass exodus to work in the morning, it became clear that something had changed. In those days, working from home was quite uncommon. Jobs that allowed such an arrangement were not known of, and most people in our community had jobs such as administration, nursing and teaching that required on-site working. Not much could be assumed from the outside but, eventually, the assumption that we didn't live the extravagant lifestyle we were used to became common knowledge. The community around us was changing too. We were not the only people with shiny things anymore.

After years of driving a modest Toyota Corolla, the parents of one of my playmates, Bradley, upgraded to a new C-Class Mercedes-Benz. We were not the only people driving a luxury car anymore. These changes also rattled our racialised imaginations, since this kind of progress unsettled the class hierarchy within the community, where those deemed blacker had access to less. Suddenly, the meaning attached to a luxury vehicle changed; it became less exclusive, in much the same way white people question the quality of education as more Black people gain access to it. In another way, it was a relief, because the attention shifted from us, and we had less to justify. There may, in fact, have been no attention on us, but our own projections of class and status caused us so much anxiety, which fuelled the need to save face. Our ego-driven class fantasy governed all our interactions with the community. My father felt that other families' upward mobility was a slight directed at him to show him up and disgrace him. They were still Boesmans in his eyes who were not accustomed to the opulence and luxury he had been the custodian of for so long. He embodied a class paranoia that manufactured all kinds of insults and attacks on him. This is the way powerful, privileged people often rationalise their need to suppress and oppress those lower down in the food chain. This was the same reasoning, though differently expressed, that drove his boss to underpay him, and yet my father could not recognise that in himself.

A Xhosa family also moved into Bernadino Heights; the first moment of integration our community had ever seen. After brief encounters with the family, everyone talked about how lovely they were. The implication of the statement was that they were not like the 'other' Black people living in townships and informal settlements. They were worthy of being allowed among us and could be taught to assimilate. Just as white people did with us, we felt that other Black people were there to aspire to our way of life. Other Black people occupied a very specific, lowly place in the apartheid-inspired Coloured imagination. We still only encountered other Black people as domestic workers or cashiers or waiters. We encountered them in servitude, to us, the same way we encountered Coloured people with less proximity to whiteness.

My crèche teacher, Liezel, was one such example. It was my first experience with the violence of the racialised class hierarchy within Coloured communities. When the crèche closed due to mismanagement, Liezel was left with no choice but to do domestic work. She came to work for us once a week. She went from being my teacher, someone I respected, to an employee of my household. Though I was a child, I was the child of her employer, and by implication I ranked above her in the hierarchy. Though she was always very gentle and affectionate as a teacher, she treated me differently when she worked in our home. She assumed a position of less authority than I had known her to have. She treated me like a little boss. I found the shift to be uncomfortable.

The Xhosa family didn't stay long, and I can only imagine why. The anti-Blackness so deeply ingrained in us must have alerted them to their 'mistake'. I remember once playing in the road with some friends. The sun had started to set, and so our parents and older siblings were coming home from work. Neighbours would often come outside to talk to each other and catch up on gossip. Two neighbours who were also new were talking about the new Xhosa family and how nice they were, when one just casually remarked, 'Sy's 'n oulike k*firmeid.' I remember stopping what I was doing to look at who said it. The conversation did not stop for one second to consider the gravity of the insult that had just been passed. Not one person found it uncomfortable or offensive. It was said with such an affectionate tone that if you did not understand the language, you would think the word was a compliment. As a child, I was afraid to challenge an adult's authority, but hearing the word felt like swallowing a mouthful of boiling blood. It was scalding and ferrous in taste. A true representation of tasting hell.

My heartrate doubled almost instantly, and although I had been sweating due to play, I could feel the sweat of anxiety cover my forehead. I was young, but I knew what the word meant. Not only linguistically but socially too. My mind conjured images of people crying and pleading for mercy, praying to a dead god, drowning in rivers of blood, clawing at prison walls, having their teeth chiselled out without anaesthetic. The word still makes the hair on the back of my neck stand up – yet, on that day, nobody even flinched at the sound of it. I would have had to hear the word being uttered by many omnipotent adults in my life until I had the agency to shut them down or distance myself from them. I could offer many explanations for how my people came to be so comfortable with the horror of dehumanising those they deem other, and they exist, but none can bring justice to the victims of its violence. There is a particular kind of spiritual and psychological dissociation Coloured people must submit to, to rest so easily with anti-Blackness. It is a crime against the self too. It is a contrived form of self-mutilation to dismember African people that way when you too are an African.

The economics of anti-Blackness best shows itself within Coloured communities and the competition for resources and status. The very class anxieties my father pandered to were in large part driven by anti-Blackness, because he accepted his position within the raced class hierarchy as a Coloured person with proximity to whiteness. He accepted his role as the one who had to guard the gates of upward mobility, failing which he would lose his access to resources and his racial proxy. This is how our communities were set up, as self-sustaining spaza shops of white supremacy. We managed the divisions ourselves, ensuring that those at the top of the community never broke into white spaces while fending off those beneath them. It was also a perfect way to orchestrate the innocence of white supremacy by showing how such violence is self-inflicted. The set-up was perfectly crafted.

Though I can spend hours unpacking the cunning ideological weaponry of white supremacy, I am saddened today by how my people still have not woken up to the scheme. White supremacy is not only in the custody of white people. We use the tools created to annihilate us against ourselves too. It is also not a static ideology and evolves, like bacteria build immunity to antibiotics. The more we figure out its game, the more it will morph and change to entice us and seduce us with the fruits of inequality. We too are agents of white supremacy.

The constant competition to remain on top of the hierarchy and the internalised belief of superiority took its toll on my father. He was not only fighting for his place in the social hierarchy, but also in the family hierarchy. He had a deeply rooted need to please his own father. This was his lifelong mission. He failed many times. His life choices were never good enough for his father. His first marriage – from which my eldest sister, Gisela, was born – failed. That was a disappointment. To make it worse, he started a relationship with my mother while he was still married, another scandal. His career choice was unconventional. His life was un-Islamic. The only way he knew how to impress his father was with money. He was a man who always had money and valued his own propensity for enterprise. My father made sure that, whenever he visited his father, he left him with a wad of cash. It still wasn't enough, and I believe this unfulfillment kept my father chasing status and money his entire life. It was not a desire driven by affirmation but by anxiety. I still don't know what was going on in his mind when he lost himself to alcohol, but after my grandfather died, there would be times when my father would descend into a state of near delirium and start crying about his late parent.

He cried about how unfairly his mother was treated. I have heard the story about how, one rainy day in Cape Town, my grandmother was walking home with two full hands of grocery bags. My grandfather saw her walking but drove by. When she arrived home, she asked whether he had seen her, to which he replied yes. She asked why he didn't stop to give her a ride and, coldly, he replied, 'Because you would have wet my seats.' My father never forgave this cruelty.

He also cried about how he was never good enough for his father. It was a strange sight to see my father cry, but the tears of my terrorist never moved me much. To me it was all a pretence from someone I never knew to have an emotional range that extended beyond misery and anger. There were reasons for his drinking, which was yet to reach its peak, that he could not explain to me. I doubt he tried to rationalise it for himself. Without knowing it, I saw the effects of patriarchy on my father. He was fully incarcerated in an emotional and mental prison. Having internalised the responsibility of the sole breadwinner after prohibiting my mother from working, he took on a burden he could not bear. His yearning for his father's admiration and respect kept him locked in a constant state of trepidation. Although he loved his mother dearly, it was his father's admiration and respect that he valued. What it meant to be a man was unbearable yet non-negotiable. Though the benefits accrued, I believe with a different set of sensibilities, my father would have chosen a different life, hence he decided to escape through the neck of a whisky bottle. He would rather poison his body than live fully present.

Many men lived the way he did. Very few men in our community lived life unaided. In fact, men and women alike could not get through life without help. Many wives kept themselves comfortably sedated with alcohol as they went through their daily lives. Resigned to living under their husbands' thumbs. Today, still, we can't wait for the weekend to escape the drudgery of unfulfilling lives. Perhaps it was because it affected my life so directly that I separated my father's dysfunction from what was happening all around me – but everyone was trying to escape. I knew nobody who drank alcohol for the enjoyment. Almost everyone smoked to calm their nerves.

In one form or another, everyone was experiencing assisted living.

I often marvel at our longevity, despite all the ways in which we have to compromise our bodies just to make it through life with some joy. If not cut short by unnatural events, we live long lives for everything we have gone through. It makes me wonder just how much truth there is in all the healthy living doctrines we are sold. That too has something to gain from us buying the providence of the earth at a premium. It seems we are more valuable to healthy living than it is to us. I suspect that these realisations dawned on us a long time ago, but without the language to expose its violence, we chose to flee from it.

My father lived a long life in spite of himself. I always say, if there is one good thing that came out of his life, it is that he taught me what *not* to be. My father never sat me down to teach me anything about life. He simply lived his life in front of me and left me to figure it out. Both Tayshira and I became overachievers. I chose to do it through academics, and she chose enterprise. Though it was seen as admirable, this level of hyperfunctioning tends to get us into the same trouble that inspired our choices in the first place. Escape, again, becomes the only option. My family has a long history of escapism.

With all this pressure and his propensity for escapism, my father had spiritually vacated the home. Without the requirement to be at a workplace, he was at liberty to do what he wanted. He was always armed with bravado, which he expressed as invincibility. He could drink at any time of the day, any day of the week. Sometimes, he would even do his work while drunk and, for some reason, all his colleagues were so accommodating. I think their compassion was largely driven by me and my mother, who were wholly dependent on his income. People tolerated his indiscretions for our sake. We always said my father was protected by association with us. It didn't matter how many times he offended people and how many bridges he burnt; within the textile industry, the doors were always open to him. Always another chance.

Life remained on autopilot for some time. We seemed to have regained a level of stability and comfort, and the fretting about finances abated. Things were back to as normal as they could be, and I think I started to try and live around my father. I had to learn to stop expecting something new from the same old person. I was trying to believe my father when he showed me who he was. In the meantime, like my mother, I enjoyed material comforts as much as I could. I knew I could easily appeal to my father's ego as the provider when he was drunk, so I would use his drinking sprees to ask for things I wanted. Whether it was a new pair of sneakers for casual day at school or money for a new CD that had just been released, I could get anything I wanted. It was also the only time I knew I would see some form of affectionate care from my father and not be shrugged off. Not that he wouldn't agree to my requests when he was sober, but it would always come with a demoralising comment or an unnecessary insult.

The contrived relationship I developed with his dysfunction could be described as affectionate manipulation. This form of entanglement with dysfunction endured until I was an adult. It was my only chance at having a relationship with my father that didn't constantly make me feel unwanted. I realised that if I weren't going to stop him, I would have to find a way to live with him and derive some joy from life too. There was a time when I believed that my father did not care for me, even though during every drunken stupor he would find the courage to profess his love for me. Through the haze of fumes, all I saw was an actor emulating the script of real life. My father probably never heard the words 'I love you' from either of his parents. In fact, he would often tell me that, while he was growing up, something he heard often in his home was that children 'should be seen and not heard'. I can only imagine what the experience of trying to abide by that must have been like for a young child. To be made an intruder in the only home you know. If that was his experience of childhood, then I am sure that he believed he was giving us better. At least he was there for us to see. We knew where our father was. We were allowed a voice in our home, even if it was sometimes regulated. My father knew that he had to find a way to show his love, but he had no tools at his disposal. He chose material goods as his conduit. The loss of language when it comes to communicating love is one of the most violent dispossessions still evident in Coloured families. The long shadow of harm follows many of us who have not yet lifted our heads to see where the sun is. My father stood in the middle of that shadow, thinking he was protecting us from the harshness of the sun.

Love, I have learnt, is a matter of perspective.

Nine

After finishing school, Tayshira elected to study at Varsity College. At her graduation dinner, she invited a few friends. At the end of the dinner, before going out with her friends, she introduced her boyfriend, Dominic, to my father. He was tall and very dark skinned. My father just looked at him like he was an insect. Nobody was good enough for his daughter, but especially not a dark-skinned boy. That introduction set their entire relationship.

In 2001, Tayshira applied for a working holiday in London. At the time, the UK issued visas that allowed you to work and live in the country for a limited time. My father helped her with all the arrangements. Being Tayshira, though, she wired some of the money my father had given her to Dominic, because he was to join her. Yet another stunt. My father was furious, but eventually everything was arranged, and she went to London for two years. Upon returning in 2003, with little to show for it, finding a job in Cape Town proved too difficult given her urgent need for independence. A cousin of ours had just moved to Johannesburg, and upon hearing there were more opportunities, Tayshira decided to move there. As had happened with London, Dominic followed. This time, Tayshira cashed in the money she got for a plane ticket to buy two bus tickets for them to travel together.

On the evening they left, my mom had prepared a Tupperware with frikkadels, egg sandwiches, samoosas and roast chicken. There may have been a flask of soup involved too. Padkos is a Coloured tradition that translates pure love. Even though it wasn't that long ago, buying food while travelling long distances by road was quite unheard of, even for those who could afford it. It's not what we do. Taking the well wishes, prayers and travelling mercies of loved ones along in a Tupperware still constitutes traditional Coloured road travel. Food sharing in Coloured communities is a love language, and every little bit counts. When my brother Yusuf made his way to London two years after Tayshira led the way, some neighbours showed up with home-cooked meals for him to take on the plane. When he told them he could not take it on the plane, they were visibly distraught.

After Tayshira had been in Johannesburg for a year, my mother and I were ready for a visit. We were ecstatic at the thought of our first flight to anywhere. The furthest my mother and I had ever been was Port Elizabeth – by car – and I was too young to remember that trip. Just to know what it feels like to sit in a plane was thrilling. As a child, I always marvelled at planes when they flew overhead. They were even more magical at night with their flickering lights that resembled Christmas lights. While watching a plan overhead at night, I would be flying to New York in my head.

Although he paid for the tickets, because there was no way he would allow anyone else to take that power away from him, my father begrudged our visit to Tayshira. He despised Dominic. He despised the fact that he was living off his daughter. She was the one earning the money, anchoring them with security. By my father's estimation, Dominic was in a delayed adolescence and trying his hand at every get-rich-quick scheme he could find.

This objection could still be understood, but my father also despised Dominic for his dark skin, which was completely out of line. Completely outraged, my mother and I got into many fights with my father to defend Dominic against that all-too-familiar anti-Black colourism upheld by Cape Muslims and, in particular, Indians. My grandfather was himself flagrantly racist and normalised such dehumanising discourses, with no resistance from anyone. There is a culture of racist anti-Blackness that is well and alive among Cape Muslims but also Muslims in other parts of the country and the world. It is not a teaching of Islam but it certainly is a very popular form of shared culture. Even Coloured Muslims, who under different political circumstances would understand themselves as Black, subscribe to the prejudice.

The often-irrelevant retort for justifying the use of South Africa's most notorious racial slur against Black people has its root in Arabic. When trying to downplay the harm caused by the word, this link to Arabic is invoked, but it is exactly this link that provides an insight into the racist social complex among Muslims. The complexity stems from the classification of non-Muslims as Al-Kafirun (the disbelievers), but upon closer inspection and from personal experience, I realised that the word's tentacles grew to interchange non-human with non-believer. So, the 'k*firs' and the 'Boesmans' became the non-believers, and the non-believers were always the 'k*firs' and the 'Boesmans'. In this matrix, racism and religious imperialism melted into each other to form an indistinguishable mass of discrimination. The unbelievable thing was that white and Indian people would call us Boesmans, and yet we would use it for other Coloured people who didn't fit the profile of Cape Malay Muslims. This is how Muslims have camouflaged their racism and anti-Blackness with semantics. In this way, Islam also became an unwitting tool to further maintain structural white supremacy within our communities and keep adding more layers to the contrived social structure we already occupied. Through Muslim, anti-Black racism you could easily see just how dependent racism and racial prejudice is on power. We were mongrels and oriental sorcerers in the white world but purveyors of white supremacy in our own worlds.

The day my mother and I left for Johannesburg, my father made sure he was completely out of it. He behaved as if someone had died. Besides his distrust of Dominic, I think he also felt that we were betraying him by wanting to visit Tayshira. We had grown accustomed to this behaviour. We were prepared for his sulking long before the day of departure arrived.

My father consistently beckoned alliances within the family, where he was the centre of contention. Anybody who didn't agree with his position was exiled to disownment. It became quite comical how he would disown one of us nearly every week, on rotation. The weight of the word has lost all substance since. I sometimes think about all the arguments that have played out over the years and recognise a commitment to discord. My mother always placates every painful memory with 'There were good times too,' in an effort to escape the magnitude of a life overshadowed by discord. Yes, there were good times, but such times were so exceptional that you can only assume that we were invested in turmoil. I think about the generational trauma that both my parents lived through, from forced removals to substance abuse, and wonder if maybe trauma has been their only form of communication. Perhaps the warped comfort and familiarity of trauma became so soothing that when there was an opportunity to live without it, they ran the other way or recreated it. There would be real opportunities to handle disagreements with care and kindness, but somehow all of them would devolve into a competition to see who could be the most hurtful. Sometimes, there would be nothing going on, and someone would orchestrate a fight. We joked about that too, saying the aggressor is bored and craves a fight, but it was not funny. We have dragged each other through hell and back for all our flaws and shortcomings, never letting the other forget just how imperfect they are. We do not know how to foster familial intimacy based on love and respect but communicate through wounding. We poke and scratch at each other's wounds as a way of saying we see the pain. Maybe we are looking for a portal into each other's hearts, and the easiest entrance is through an existing hole. Whatever it is, the cycle of trauma has shaped our relationships, and unlearning will take many hours and claim many unassuming, innocent casualties. When we bleed on others, we transfer that trauma. It's like dropping raw rice on the floor. Recovering every grain is near impossible and, as time goes by, you keep finding grains you didn't know you had lost in the first place. Healing has been an inconclusive journey.

WE DIDN'T ALLOW MY FATHER to spoil our mood, so we asked a friend of my mother to drop us off. Although, whenever we went away, my mother and I worried about the potential harm my father could bring to himself while drunk. There were times when we would stay at home just to supervise him. Resentful as we were, we could not stand the thought of him being severely harmed, and we also no longer had medical aid. The consequences of a severe injury were just too burdensome. A decision like the one to go to Johannesburg for seven days took a lot of second guessing and convincing. We realised that we had to strike a balance between babysitting a grown man and living our own lives, so we closed our eyes and left.

I was dressed to the nines for my first flight; I wore a black shirt with splashes of white that resembled dripping paint. The flight was meant to take off at 1.30pm but, just as we were about to board, a delay was announced, due to notorious thunderstorms in Johannesburg. What was meant to be an afternoon flight became an evening flight, only taking off at 9pm.

I was enthralled by the inside of the cabin – I could not believe that I was on a plane. I had chosen a window seat to make sure I could look out of the window and see what the earth looked like from above. I wanted to see the clouds up close. Flying was a magical experience. Finally, I was inside one of those planes that flew overhead with the Christmas lights. Life couldn't get any better. When we arrived around 11pm, Dominic was waiting at arrivals to receive us. I felt as if I was in a new country. I loved 'Joburg' instantly and could not wait to visit, again and again.

Though we were both happy to be away, my mom could not help but check in on my father every now and then. She did it partly out of concern for his well-being and partly out of worry that he would damage things in the house. Unlike me, she battled to detect his level of sobriety over the phone. Unless he was completely unable to form his words properly, my mother was eager to believe that he was sober. Her eternal naivety, her belief that somehow he would maintain contact with the real world while we were away, kicked in. I thought about him, but I was too happy to be away from home to act on my thoughts. I knew what I would find if I did check in, and I didn't want to be disappointed.

When we landed back in Cape Town, one of my mother's cousins picked us up from the airport. We arrived in the early afternoon on a clear and sunny day. We asked her to drop us in front of the house and leave. We didn't know what we would find, so thought it best not to expose her to what could have been a potentially disturbing sight. All the shutters were closed, which meant that the house was completely dark inside – a bad sign. Although my father liked to shut the light out in summer, because it kept the house cool, completely closed shutters in the middle of the day seemed a bit extreme. We approached with caution. My mother tried to open the front door, but it was locked. No movement could be seen through the frosted glass panels on the door. She knocked.

After a minute or so, a shadow emerged on the other side of the door. The door opened to reveal a stranger. A semi-naked man with a full white beard and dishevelled white-grey hair stood and looked at us with beady eyes. He looked as if he had been exposed to the elements for some time. We were truly frightened. The stranger was indeed my father, completely unrecognisable. He had obviously not shaven or bathed since we had left seven days before. The house smelt like it had not had fresh air circulate through it for a week. It smelt of cigarette ash, dust, whisky and fermenting garbage. After opening the door, my father turned right around to his room and closed the door. My mother and I immediately started opening the shutters and windows to let light and air in. We also wanted to see what the house looked like, since we were certain that nothing had been swept or wiped in seven days. Considering what my father looked like when he opened the door, I was curious to know how much he had been drinking to let go of his grooming to that extent. I walked into the yard to check the municipal refuse bin. On top of a few black bags was a layer of green glass made up of seven empty bottles of J&B whisky. That amounted to drinking an average of one bottle of whisky on each day we were away. I was astounded that one person's body could take that much alcohol without caving into alcohol poisoning or some form of shock. This was by far the worst I had seen.

I felt bad for my mother. To see the man she loved reduced – by self-mutilation – to a shadow of who she met. She always told me how handsome he was when she met him and how hypnotised she was by his beauty. I wondered how it must feel to watch the person with whom you imagined active partnership cop out on you.

There was only so much comfort I could provide for her before the company of a teenage child proved inadequate. I'm sure she sometimes wanted to go for walks on the beach or date-night dinners with her husband but, when he wasn't drunk, he was agitated and abrupt. I don't think I ever saw them in the embrace of romance. For as long as I could remember, my parents had always been two people, sharing a house and children. Seeing my father look like a mutation of the abominable snowman must have broken my mother's heart. Many married women of her generation resigned themselves to mechanical marriages centred on their husband's ego. The vitality of these marriages depended on how affirmed the husband felt. These arrangements were normalised as respectable lives that affirmed traditional family values. They were microcosms of societal hierarchies that sorted people according to their assigned human value.

My mother was such a free spirit, and at times rebellious. Her confinement to what seemed like such an unfulfilling, unequitable arrangement saddened me. The utter powerlessness further compounded by my presence was painful to watch. I was my mother's companion but also the albatross around her neck at times. If she ever wanted to leave my father, even temporarily, I was always the reason why she would have to go back.

When my father woke up from his hangover slumber, he would always try and pretend that nothing had happened while seeing us visibly upset and disapproving. This time, after grooming himself back to a state of recognisability, he came to talk to us and ask what's wrong.

'Daddy, you drank seven bottles of whisky in seven days! How can you ask what's wrong?' I asked.

He didn't respond much during such conversations.

'Farouk, this is out of hand. You can't go on like this. We can't live like this.'

My mother had said this so many times before, but her words moved very little in a man who had once told her he would never stop drinking because otherwise she would have no problems.

Through all of these drinking sprees, despite having developed diabetes a few years earlier, my father got a clean bill of health upon every visit to the doctor. Even our family doctor said he was a medical mystery. He had not one alcohol-related illness, and his diabetes remained under control. At some point, we even thought the doctor was conspiring with him to fool us, but everything was verifiably sound.

After our conversation, my father agreed to get medical help for his addiction. He was going to get on Antabuse – a tablet that, when taken, would make you unbearably ill if it interacted with alcohol. It seemed fool proof.

But we ended up the fools being proofed. The charade lasted for about a week before my father was back at it, Antabuse and all. Disappointed but not surprised, I realised that nothing about the situation at home was going to improve in my last years of high school.

At the end of my Grade 11 year, I was elected treasurer of the student council. In old terms, that was deputy head boy. The night of the prizegiving ceremony where we were announced, I also received multiple academic and cultural awards. I had come a long way from primary school. Since my Grade 8 year, I consistently improved, climbing up the academic ladder. That night, I received full colours for culture and half colours for academics. I felt proud of myself for achieving all of this in spite of all the distractions. All the parents of the new student council members were called to the bottom of the stage to pin our badges for us. I saw everyone's parents come in pairs. My mother appeared from the crowd, beaming. She was so happy and proud to be *that* parent, yet again. It was just the two of us again. We shared all our victories and breakdowns alone. We knew what that moment meant for both of us. We were entering the final leg of the race as victors, and we still had each other to rely on.

In my matric year, I had reached the peak of my academic excellence. I maintained one of the highest average percentages throughout the year, fluctuating between position one and two in the academic rankings. Academic excellence protected me from a lot of homophobic bullying in high school. Other kids snickered and mocked me behind my back but had to respect my excellence. They also knew to keep me close as a resource when they scrambled to do their homework before school started and they needed help or sometimes to copy mine. A part of me wants to believe they also genuinely liked me regardless of my sexuality, and some did, but being gay was never fun growing up. I hid behind my academics too. When the questions about girlfriends came around, my response was always that I had no time for girls because I was focusing on my academics. Secretly I had crushes on some of the boys at school. It was all I knew, and that was enough for me.

After my March exams, I realised that no matter how hard I tried, I just didn't get accounting. So, I decided to switch from higher to standard grade accounting. The switch caused me to lose exemption, which would allow me entry into university. I only realised this when I applied to Stellenbosch University for provisional acceptance and received a letter saying that I did not qualify to apply because I did not have exemption. I could not believe it. I was shattered at the thought of not going to university after everything. My mother came to talk to the school, and Mrs Boshoff, a teacher who took a liking to me, pitched in to help. She never taught me, but Mrs Boshoff still took it upon herself to personally liaise with the university on my behalf and make a case for why I should be granted senate discretionary admission. As an alumnus of the university, she knew how to talk the talk. She wrote a heartfelt letter selling all my hard work, agreeable character and suitability for an institution of such prestige. Interestingly, one of her arguments was that I did not belong at the University of the Western Cape, because I was 'too refined and well rounded'. I didn't realise the code she was sending with that statement, but it surely cracked the senate of one of the oldest and ostensibly most racist institutions in South Africa. I was accepted on condition that I produced the stipulated results in my matric final exams.

I passed matric at the top of my class. I had the highest average percentage in the grade and was named the Dux learner. I was elated – and finally, after all those years, my father also thought I was worth celebrating. He too was affirmed by my achievement. Academics were everything to him, and especially achievement in natural science. Passing matric is an achievement in Coloured communities because it was not a given that you would finish school. Neither of my father's parents finished school. My grandfather only had a Standard 1 education, while both my mother's parents didn't make it to high school. My mother only went as far as Standard 8 before she had to find work. Completing school has never been a guarantee in my family and, for many, tertiary education was a dream.

Image was also very important when it came to education. During apartheid, the options for what Coloured people could become were mostly limited to teachers, nurses and artisans. Those were the roles – caregivers and builders – we were allocated by the colonial-apartheid complex. Those roles were not inherently menial, but funnelling us into those professions had a particular kind of logic – that we were more receptive than other Black people of being tutored into white respectability. So, when I made my programme choices for university, I was strictly instructed to choose a real degree, now that we could study anything. My heart's desire was to study drama and theatre. I truly enjoyed the performing arts, and, judging by all my accolades, I clearly had a talent for it. But my mother emphatically refused to endorse that decision. My father always wanted me to become a scientist. I resented their rigidity at the time, but history would bring me to understand the power of stigma attached to us.

When my enslaved ancestors were brought to South Africa by force, they were earmarked to be cooks, artisans, entertainers and jesters. Their talents became stigmatised as a mark of servitude and foolishness. The colonial memory stretches far back and carries this shame with it. A propensity for the creative arts among people like me has always had meanings of frivolity and instability attached to it. I would only find the space to explore my creative talents after gaining legitimacy through the validation of studying science. I applied to law, physiotherapy and human life sciences with psychology. I had settled on becoming a clinical psychologist, so in the end I accepted a place in the human life sciences programme. The affirmation of my choice to pursue a scientific professional career soon made me forget about my loss of performance art as a career option.

The only thing left to do was to enjoy the matric holidays. For a while, I basked in the glory of having finished school. I was facing a new and exciting life as a university student – something exceptional in my community. I had a real shot at building a respectable life, as I was expected to. I was the pride of my parents who lapped up the honour of having a university student for a child. I was ready to make a difference in the world and please all the expectations placed on me. I was going to be a big deal; I could feel it.

Ten

The day I arrived at Stellenbosch University with my mother to register for my degree, it was as if we were both enrolling. We walked the road to this milestone, hand in hand. University was an exciting yet intimidating prospect. I had never set foot on a university campus before, and I had no frame of reference for what to expect. The first thing that struck me was that there were no gates like you find at schools. There was no distinction between the town and the university. The town's roads ran through the university. The university was not confined to one building named 'University', as I expected. How was I to know where I was and where to go if everything wasn't in one place? I was completely overwhelmed by the sheer magnitude of the campus, and I had only seen a section of it.

There was much more to see, but walking around in 40° Celsius Boland heat – in jeans – was not the smartest thing to do. My explorations would have to wait for another day.

I was not ready to leave my mother's care yet, so I opted to travel into campus and back every day. We lived 20 kilometres away, so the journey was easily managed. It was like a continuation of school, except that I had about 28 000 fellow students, and I had no idea who my teachers were, and there were no prospects of getting to know them.

The week before classes started, we were invited to partake in orientation week. New and returning students settled into their residences, and for those who stayed off campus, there were societies, clubs and private student organisations. These PSOs were created for students who didn't live at res to be able to participate in campus culture. It seemed like a good idea to join one and find a base to operate from and make some friends while on campus. Student leaders from various PSOs were stationed throughout the student centre, which was like a really small shopping mall in the middle of the campus called the Neelsie. It was named after some historical figure relevant to Afrikaner culture. I signed up to a PSO called 'Pieke' – named after the twin peaks of the Stellenbosch mountain range. We were told to meet in one of the academic buildings at a stipulated time, where we would be able to learn more about what to expect.

After getting lost, as would be the standard for the first few weeks on campus, I arrived at an old lecture theatre clad almost entirely in wood. The sight of only white men made me want to run back out, but I kept my composure. I was already drenched in sweat from walking around in the heat, but the discomfort of being in a room with them made it worse. What struck me was just how comfortable they all seemed. They appeared to have full command and ownership of the space and did not seem to be in need of anything. I could not imagine them feeling anything amiss – after all, if they looked around, they saw their own mirror images reflected back at them. Nothing was strange.

The leaders stood up and started presenting the PSO ins and outs to us. They spoke to us as if we were all returning students, despite everyone clearly being new first-year students. When I looked at the people around me, they were confirming that they were indeed familiar with that was being said. I soon realised that these first-year students were mostly children of establishment who lived in the town. They had parents and siblings who were students there, and they were already well acquainted with campus life. This was all just a formality to them. The orientation was more a welcoming to those who already knew how things worked. I was even more out of place. To end off the meeting, we were taught a song called 'Save Tonight' by Eagle-Eye Cherry. It sounded like an American country song to me. The song would be sung at an event later that evening. We were to go to a women's residence and serenade them before engaging in what was called skakel.

What was sold as a networking session was literally a cult-like mating dance where the men went to seek prospective wives on the first night on campus. This is something that would happen many times throughout the year as an approved form of student socialisation. The idea of being forced to connect with a woman with the intent of kindling a romantic association had me gasping for air. I had always found comfort in the company of girls as friends, because that's all I saw them as. The terrifying part was that most of the women also seemed to be in on the cult and were expecting men who would woo them. I was not willing nor capable of doing anything they expected. I had not even tried to woo boys, what was I to do with girls?

I wanted to leave and never come back, but I felt like I had already been committed to the plan for the night and couldn't back out. We visited Irene residence, where one of my friends from high school was placed. I stayed with her the entire night to avoid having to talk to anyone else. I couldn't wait for the nightmare to be over. When we eventually finished, I vowed never to partake in any more campus activities. I was there to get a degree, and that was it.

This was my first introduction to the power of heteronormativity in the adult world. The system around which a university-sanctioned match-making exercise was organised did not for one second consider that some students are not heterosexual. Further, it did not consider that some students had no interest in finding a mate while there. The assumption that pairing young adults in marriage-like arrangements was so commonplace – at a university of all places – that I had to wonder what service we were being offered by the establishment. From this example, it is easy to see what is meant by 'systemic' when people talk about oppression and prejudice.

The tacit endorsement of such practices as acceptable – and even desirable – shows just how heteronormative patriarchy governs from a place way above where we tend to set our sights. I realised that university was not going to be as freeing for me as it appeared to be for others. I was not even seen, at all.

Attending classes was hardly any better. The first lecture I attended was physics. The first thing the lecturer told us was that 30 per cent of us would pass the class, and some of us will drop out at the end of the year. It was as if he were hoping that the 70 per cent would leave the class, so that he could work only with the winners. I left the class convinced that I would be one of the failures and was already hatching a plan to tell my parents that I was dropping out. I also had to tell Beverley Fanella, the woman who recruited me to Stellenbosch and gave me a bursary, that her faith in me was misplaced. Beverley's office was always open to all of the overwhelmed and bewildered first years. She talked me down from the ledge and advised me to seek counselling at the university's counselling unit. She also facilitated my access to a tutor for some of my subjects.

The counselling lasted for only two sessions though. The experience of speaking to a white person who had no way of understanding why my feelings of anxiety and being overwhelmed were not simply a product of being in a new environment ... She didn't understand the effects of history, my home life and the intimidating whiteness of the academy on me. Beverley, on the other hand, knew exactly what I was talking about. She knew what it was like to have a tumultuous relationship with a parent and how it felt to have an entire legacy riding on your shoulders. She knew me and my life. She was not only available as a mentor but also as a person who shared my experiences. We developed a great friendship in her office, and with her support I resolved to persevere, not only for myself but for all the confidence placed in me. The power of affirmation from one of your own can never be understated.

Despite all of the support – or perhaps because of it – I was still feeling pressured to hide my sexuality. I leaned hard on my religion. Despite feeling outcasted and side-lined by Muslims because of the un-Islamic environment I grew up in and the disillusionment with the institution of religion, I still hoped to appease god. I was also desperate to reconcile my sexuality with the Qur'an. A Qur'an I could not comprehend but only recite.

My brother Yusuf, who ventured into religious fundamentalism a few years before I went to university, had recently married and left behind a translated Qur'an. It had been neatly tied up in a white cotton bag in the floating cupboard above my bedroom door, like a magical talisman with unspoken power meant to protect and terrify its bearer at the same time. As much as I was drawn to it in my search for validation, or perhaps damnation, I avoided it. The last glimmer of hope for a logical god who did not create someone only to condemn them drew me to investigate my position in the queue to paradise.

I browsed through the book with its delicate pages that resembled cigarette paper. Not that I could receive it at the time, but maybe it was a sign that what I was about to read was more suited to being smoked up at a New Year's Eve party than to internalise as a guide for my own spiritual and moral principles. There was talk of killing and stoning and confining for people like me, or at least the person I would eventually become. It was for the act of homosexuality, or the perversion called sodomy, that such punishment was prescribed, and not the desire for it. Through that loophole many have justified the expectation that gay Muslims were to shut off same-sex desires and commit to a life of celibacy or mindless heterosexuality.

Queer bodies are often the site of sacrifice. It is a romanticised sacrifice that feeds the ferocious hunger of the heterosexual gaze. The thought of seeing us deprived of the liberties of everyday existence adds just the right amount of distance between us to sate the heterosexual imagination. We are tolerated in faith communities and the societies their power produces for as long as we are willing to denounce our access to desire. To desire and to be desired as queer bodies is to illuminate the insecurity that keeps heterosexual desire shackled to inequality. To be observed in such freedom has the potential to inspire sexual revolution everywhere where sexuality is repressed. Queer desire is limitless in the configurations it can demand of queer bodies. In a world built on inequality, limitless desire is a threat to power.

After walking headfirst into the hornet's nest that was the Qur'an, I decided to focus on the things that could comfort me. It is said that fasting during the month of Ramadan accrues to the abiding Muslim abundant blessings amounting to a near-guaranteed entry into paradise in the afterlife. It is also said that Satan is held in bondage for the entire 40 days, and Muslims are therefore free of temptation as they get closer to god. If I just kept to myself and made sure I fasted, surely I would be in favour with god? I was ready to commit myself to a life of denial. Denial of desire, of thought and of bodily autonomy. It was just safer that way. That's all I really wanted – to be safe from judgement and violence at home and elsewhere.

TEST SEASON WAS UPON ME, and it happened to fall within the month of Ramadan. Fasting and studying is an unnecessary combination of bodily shock and exhaustion I would not recommend. By now a system that allows for the retroactive accumulation of spiritual blessings should have been designed if South African Muslims were serious about existing in a secular state. Writing tests at university happened around 7pm. For those who lived on campus or nearby, this posed no challenge. I had to wait around after class, and on such days could spend up to 14 hours on campus. Luckily, I had a friend who lived in a flat opposite the humanities building, so I could study and recharge there after class. Her sister would always make sure I had a proper meal to break my fast with before we had to go and write the test.

Balancing my studies and fasting was an overwhelming task that felt much more like a punishment than a blessing. Fasting on its own was always torturous to me. I could not understand god's need for seeing us in constant sacrifice and deprivation to be worthy of his approval. I was in search of salvation and could not question the merits of eternal sacrifice when it was the only lens I had through which to interpret my life. All social cues taught me that a good life, here and in the next realm, was something to be earned with hunger, broken bones and a bleeding heart. I was not entitled to ease and nurturing lest I accepted the physical and spiritual poverty that would be visited upon me in return for claiming it. I chose righteous suffering.

The legend of Satan's bondage proved futile at home. Not a single thing changed, that month or any other month thereafter. My father continued undeterred against the warnings of punishment for defiling the body during the holy month. Not even the promise of eternal paradise was enough to entice him away from escaping into the warmth of a green bottle. For some reason, although we practised nothing that was required by Islam, there was always the need to pretend that we believed in it. It was the result of believing that religion is an innate part of humans and that you cannot choose otherwise. So, after running down the list of required things we don't do as Muslims, the conclusion would always be that we are still Muslim because we are identified as such. Though we did not practise, we respected the practices, so when my father showed such blatant disrespect for the holiness of Ramadan by drinking throughout, we felt it. We might have been Waterslamse, but this was ridiculous. To me it was as if Satan were right there with me, mocking my efforts at pleasing god.

Fasting in Islam means not eating or drinking anything from sunrise to sunset. This usually means waking up somewhere between 3am and 5am, depending on the season, to eat and pray. I never did the prayers, because I didn't know how.

In Islam, there are certain conditions under which you are exempt from fasting, such as illness. So, my father couldn't fast because of his diabetes, and my mother didn't fast; she would always say it was because she had low blood pressure, but I wasn't convinced. I think she didn't care for it.

With my parents not fasting, I was the only one in our home who was. Experiencing fasting as torture made it hard enough, but to wake up to the prospect of eating alone made the hill even steeper. While everyone else in the world got to draw even closer to their families and communities through sharing food during Ramadan, I clung to my thinning faith.

My father would be floating around the house at that time. His way of trying to show affection to me would be to prepare food for me in the morning. Since high school, he would set out a breakfast of my choice with meticulous care. So meticulous that he would lay the cutlery out restaurant style, evenly spaced. The breakfast foods were arranged in order of consumption, and a glass was set on the right side in line with the edges of the placemat. I ate leisurely. However, if I didn't finish quickly enough, the hooting car in the driveway would remind me of his impatience. My disdain for his perpetual dysfunction robbed me of the capacity to appreciate his gestures of care. One morning during Ramadan, he came to wake me up to eat. He had prepared me a cooked breakfast before the fast that lay ahead. His presence, him standing over my bed, startled me. On closer inspection I realised that he was tipsy, and I became instantly angry. Not only did he disrupt my routine, but he showed such blatant disrespect for me and the holy month. I was offended.

'Why are you here? Leave me, I'm sleeping!' I erupted.

'But I made you ...'

'No! Just leave me alone!'

My father slipped away, very dejected and hurt by my outburst. Despite his perceived disrespect for Ramadan, he was genuinely supportive of my efforts to observe it. He was thoughtful enough to cook me breakfast. It really was a twisted enactment of the complexities within our relationship and, even through his demons, he tried to be a supportive father. I think by this stage he started reflecting on our life together and the lost years between us.

There had been many arguments and accusations between us stating clearly my feelings of rejection and emotional abandonment. Since I was five years old my father had been telling me that he didn't have much time left on earth, but I think by the time I was at university, he had really started believing it.

Reflecting on all of this, I got up to eat the breakfast, which was an omelette, two slices of toast and a glass of juice. You had to appreciate my father's eye for aesthetics. He took such care in arranging everything perfectly for me. He thought of everything, but I would not be satisfied. I couldn't see it then, because I only wanted one thing from him, but he tried in his way to show that he cared for me. The sadness in his voice when he tried to explain his efforts to me haunts me to this day. I have felt bad about hurting him ever since. Still, I just wished he would stay sober.

My father's choices to numb himself through life were his. They served a purpose to him, and perhaps that was fair. Though he truly was a vexing presence to us, I must wonder what he would say if he felt safe to tell us why he would rather be mentally vacant than live in our company. If it was within the capacity of a child to understand the burden of generational trauma, I could have taken myself out of it and viewed my father through his own eyes. He certainly had too much responsibility, systemically and self-imposed. His investment in patriarchy shackled him to the burden of providence. He disempowered my mother by making her stay at home. Although she never had her heart set on working after she got married, she had no power to make substantial decisions for me or herself. Resigning herself to the fact that resisting her disempowerment could only get her so far, she set out to extract joy through the material things on offer. Between the three of us, a relationship motivated by guilt circulated.

My father was always having to make up for something he had done, and to show no remorse would be to reveal a callous disregard for his family. He could buy our forgiveness, so he did. It was the easiest way to see us happy and be absolved of wrongdoing for a while. It is possible that he didn't want to change and that he liked living slightly removed from reality. We have always viewed it as abnormal – but, considering the circumstances of a life struggling to manage all the expectations placed on it, escapism was a defence mechanism. If he didn't drink himself out of the drudgery of a perpetually aspirational life, he would probably have died by suicide. His lingering belief in an Abrahamic god might have been the only thing that stopped him.

Living within the confines of societal conditioning is a process of mimicking. Everyone sets a precedent on how best to follow the rules, and although they claim to be guided by some divine power, they are all after the validation of the next person. Those who receive the most validation and adoration become the best models for us to mimic. When people like my father break that system, they are termed abnormal. The question we don't ask is, 'What is normal about trying to fit into this system of injustice?'

In this period of my life, I could only see my own needs. The arrogance of youth allows very little awareness of the struggles of those around you. To balance understanding for my parents' struggles and acknowledgement of how that hurt me in the process is difficult. To learn how to speak about their lives in the context of the times while not excusing the harm they caused is a journey of empathetic self-discovery. To dismiss my own experiences of despair would be to betray myself, but to narrate my parents' experiences outside of the structures they had to submit to would be dishonest.

The subjects of generational trauma have to learn to be healers. We have to learn to understand minds, and blood, and connective tissue. We have to become the people we hate to honour the people we love. We are sailors adrift at sea balancing on 1 000-metre swells while still advising those on the shore how to assemble the life rafts needed to save us. The burden of navigating generational trauma while trying to end it weighs heavily on one's existence.

Through the white gaze we are strong and resilient – two things it can never get enough of. I had resolved later on in life to stop taking pride in strength and resilience. We are all entitled to be soft and weak. It is therapy to allow oneself softness and dependence. My life's mission after leaving my parents' home was to be fiercely independent and never need anyone for anything. It seemed like an empowering thing to do. I have since learnt that the need to be constantly strong and independent is a response to trauma. The aversion to vulnerability is a self-denial of one of the most basic human needs. It is glorious to be soft and to experience and give care, especially in the face of such a harsh existence. To create communities of care is one of the most valuable gifts we can give to ourselves. I can say this, after years of reflection.

Although it had saved me from diving headfirst into the abyss, which I believe was my father's refuge, I regret not having the vocabulary to share it with him. Maybe our relationship could have been one of consultation and not confrontation. But if I had this kind of relationship, I might not have developed the ability to be reflexive and empathetic. The trauma that is part and parcel of marginalised lives serves a convoluted purpose. We suffer for the experience of it but, through it, we might get closer to embodying the humanity we need to experience in the world. It is convoluted, because attaining humanity should not necessitate suffering.

I WOULD CONTINUE TRYING to please god for many years, offering my comfort, both physically and mentally, as sacrifices for his grace. I would suffer many insults in silence when my mother remarked how great the parents on Oprah were for accepting their queer children, as long as she didn't have to deal with it, or when my brother referred to gay men with 'Sies!' The Muslim god is a god appeased by constant self-sacrifice. A competitive god in need of constant validation. At this point, I was caught between being obliterated by the demands of Islam and the violence it enabled in its custodians. As before, I found refuge in academic excellence.

My last years of undergraduate study would put me through tests I just knew the boys in the PSO were not facing. By the end of my first year at university, I had lost almost all my campus friends to dropping out. Some dropped out because of finances, others because they could not handle the academic load. Some didn't want to study in the first place but had expectations to meet. They wanted to be DJs and entertainers but had already been betrothed to careers in medicine or accounting to bring lost honour and prestige to their families. For many of us, our lives are not our own, and negotiating our terms equates to disrespecting our families. We were not allowed the luxury of failure for fear of the potential financial ruin our families could suffer. We are insurance policies for many of our parents, and we carry the burden of lifting them out of hardship.

My generation carries a unique burden as some of the first to have a shot at success without the constraints of legislated apartheid. Our parents bought into the dream we were sold about equal opportunity for all and started banking on our ability to break through the ceilings they were not allowed to touch. Interrogating our relationship with success and opportunity will always be entangled with the politics of historical dispossession. Even when we walk those campus streets of white universities, our steps don't count the same as those of the children of the establishment. Our feet don't touch the ground.

Eleven

In my third year at university, I was on an academic winning streak. I had overcome all the intimidation of new subjects and lecturers and had a good grasp of what I was learning. I had really developed a knack for physiology – after all, I walked away with the trophy for biology in matric. I had been doing well enough in the previous two years, but that third year was important for my record to be selected for the honours programme in psychology. I could not put a foot wrong.

After two years of gruelling test and exam seasons, I got the hang of studying. I was in the thick of the mid-year exams and had made sure that my exam entrance marks were good, so that I didn't have to worry too much about the exam outcome. All my marks were high enough to make sure that I would pass all my exams. But I didn't just want to pass, I wanted to excel.

Distinctions were an important affirmation for me, after years of criticism from my father. I broke down in a fit of sobbing when he told me I could wipe my arse with a top 10 pass in Grade 10. After years of being made to feel like my efforts were not good enough, I could not take a single minute more of the abuse. I told him that that was my best and, if it weren't good enough for him, then I had nothing more to offer. He stopped after that, but his constant, unnecessary harshness had already damaged my self-esteem. I've often heard how it was his way of preparing me to face the prejudice in the world and to push me to do better. I can appreciate that, but I have never been able to excuse the violence of breaking your child's efforts down. He might have been preparing me for an unfair world that would break me down, but surely he could have found a better way. I was never going to read my father's unfair critiques of me as attempts at building my character.

Social reality is not a vaccine that you inject into your child's life with the intent of building immunity against reality. We do not win anything by internalising the violence of a society that harms us. It is for us to realise that we are being harmed and to demand an end to that violence. We have to learn to stop being the first site of violence our children encounter. There are better ways to expose them to reality that don't harm them. Not having children is another fool proof way to make sure nobody is recovering from you in their adulthood. There are options.

For me, excelling was the only option. I was working with an 80 per cent class mark for my mid-year physiology exam and feeling confident and comfortable. I was the type of student who was always ahead of schedule with my studies. Each subject was allocated seven days of studying, so that by the time the exam came around, I would be cruising through revision. I had a highly efficient and meticulous system worked out. Needless to say, I valued preparation in a world that was so predictable and stable. I was yet to learn just how much chaos life can send your way to throw all your preparation off the edge of a cliff.

Two days before the exam, I was still studying. I used Tayshira's old room to study, so that I felt like I was elsewhere. My father was floating around the house as usual, mumbling to himself. I would hear him occasionally call my mother, probably for no reason, but for the rest the house was generally calm. I couldn't pay attention to the atmosphere, which continued to be gloomy. My attention was focused on the PowerPoint slides in front of me. By third year, we didn't use textbooks all that much, even though we had them for reference, but relied on the slides the lecturers presented to us. My method was to read the slides and make notes of the most important points. Once I had captured them all, I would use my notes to cement what I had studied on my revision days. I was set on passing this exam with a significant distinction.

The door opened. My father, a swaying tower of intoxicated anger, appeared. His face resembled that of a Spanish bull just before it is about to impale the matador with its horns for teasing it too long. As if the red cloth were being waved in front of me, an instant anger overcame me. Upon looking at his face, I could see he was looking for a fight. He wanted to know what I was doing in the room. His tone was accusatory. He was trying to involve me in an argument he had with my mother. I wasn't getting involved this time. I knew it would end badly.

'Daddy, I'm studying, leave me alone!'

He persisted in taunting me until I screamed for him to get out. The anger unhinged me. He kept on, taunting and insulting me, until I lost control and slammed my hand into my laptop keyboard to release my frustration. I was done with holding back. I stood up and grabbed him by his shoulders, turned him around and marched him out of the room. I turned back and slammed the door – locking it in nearly one sweep. I was panting.

What happened was more than just the usual argument I had with my father about his drinking. I was so moved by the power he had to taunt me that I lost control of my temper and manhandled my father. I was devastated that it had gone that far. I was taught to respect my mother and my father, so that the days of my life would be lengthened.

But do parents not also have a responsibility not to put their children through absolute hell? I had never heard a sermon about parents' responsibility to their children.

My fate was about to get worse. I looked down at the computer to try and continue studying. It was blank. It would not respond to any inputs. Like me, it was just blank. I could not continue studying. Even if the computer switched on, studying for that day had been ruined. I was never going to be ready in time for the exam. I needed more study time, and fixing the computer was not going to happen in a day. I went to my mother to ask her what I should do. I was hopeless.

We had no choice but to go to our family doctor and explain the situation to him, so that he could give me a sick note. He knew our family struggle with alcoholism better than anyone. He was always supportive. He had the ability to distinguish between what is unethical and what is humane. Sometimes doing the humane thing means breaking the rules, and he would have given me a sick note, so that I could write the supplementary exam. When my mother called the surgery, as Murphy would have it, our doctor wasn't in. She booked an appointment with a new doctor we had never met before. She had joined the practice a few months earlier. I didn't even know what she looked like, and she knew nothing about me. I was much more than the information contained in my folder. She couldn't possibly understand.

When we arrived at the doctor's waiting rooms, I was a knot of distress. There were no guarantees, and I had no backup plan. When my name was called, I looked up to see a blonde, white woman. Her hair was cut into a severe tapered bob, and she had a stern expression. Things were already off to a bad start. My mother and I shimmied into her office as she stood with her outstretched arm offering an awkward welcome. It seemed as if she had to constantly remind herself to be welcoming of her patients.

'What can I do for you?' she asked with the tone of a corporate executive.

I was too intimidated to speak, but my mother encouraged me to spit it out.

'My dad … I'm at Stellenbosch … I have an exam … my laptop …'

I doubt I was able to offer any coherent account of the events that led me to her consulting room, but after stumbling between me and my mother, we got the message out.

'I can't do that. That would be a breach of my ethical code. I understand your problem, but there's nothing I can do. I cannot lie.'

I was amazed. People lie every day with the sole intention of harming others, and nothing happens to them. All I needed was for someone to use their power to help me defend myself against the power of another uncaring system. What I was coming to realise was that I was trying to use the power of one system to protect myself against a system it was related to. They all look out for each other, and I couldn't blame her for looking out for herself. In theory, I was asking her to risk her professional reputation for no gain. I had nothing to offer her in return.

I was distraught. I knew I wouldn't be able to nail the exam the way I wanted to. Even the work I had already studied was fuzzy behind all my rage. Whatever revision I could still do wasn't going to help, since I had lost my will to work. What was the point of working hard if I had no power to resist my circumstances that conspired to derail my efforts? All I heard throughout my life was that if I worked hard I would be rewarded. The statement had no provisos or qualifiers like 'Unless your father is a menacing drunkard hellbent on sabotaging your efforts'. The dark, smoky corners of society that produce these statements do not reflect our realities. It is a privilege to do so little and still succeed.

On the morning of my exam, I was a morose shadow. I was the lamb preparing to go to the slaughterhouse. I had no choice but to go, knowing fully I was to meet my demise.

But somewhere I still had an audacity pulsing through me. I had a strategy to make sure I tackled the questions I could answer confidently first to save time to ruminate over creative responses for the ones I was less confident about. For the first time in a long time, I ran out of time to finish the paper and left out an entire 25-mark question. I remember writing a little note for the lecturer to soothe the disappointment I anticipated, since I had been such an active student in class.

But there was no point in brooding over it.

When my marks came back, it was worse than I expected. I got 58 per cent. My exam mark had to be extremely bad to take a class mark of 80 per cent down to 58 per cent.

My anger resurfaced. I had made peace with the outcome when I walked out of the exam, but being disappointed all over again when I saw the mark reminded me of how I got there. I passed, but not with the mark I wanted. It was not the goal I set for myself. I wanted better for myself, and I was denied that. It was not supposed to happen that way in the first place.

I was even more angry about the fact that when my father saw my results, he would probably question why that mark was so low. I realised that trying to pursue this dream in which my father finally wanted to be a functional parent was futile. I would be hurting myself for the rest of my life with that expectation.

I became completely withdrawn from any interactions with him. He wouldn't even notice anyway. I had lost faith in everything, including Islam, which I'd still hoped would save me from the embarrassment and misery of my father's chaos.

MORE SCEPTICAL THAN I was before, I still tried to go to mosque on Fridays for Jumu'ah prayers. When I reached puberty and was considered mukallaf and responsible for my spirituality, it was expected of me to go to mosque on Fridays. All the Muslim boys at school used to leave early to go to mosque, and I would be asked why I wasn't leaving with them. It had become the easiest way to determine how committed I was to Islam. There was still a standing inquiry into my level of piety, from Muslims and non-Muslims alike. It never wore off. The inquiry was more than just an attempt to shame me. It was a mirror image of the superiority Muslims often projected onto non-Muslims as judgement. In return, we were held to the standard of infallibility we claimed to adhere to and judged harshly when we faltered. It is through this dynamic of projection and reflection that people like me floundered in the crossfire and were reduced to the status of Waterslamse. The judgement I faced for shattering the image of infallibility was often worse from within the Muslim community than from outside. Nevertheless, I thought that if I could fulfil the bare minimum requirement of appropriate optics, I could find some peace.

My turning point with Islam came on a highly symbolic Good Friday. I was on a mid-year break from university and visiting my brother in Strandfontein for the weekend. He was still highly fanatical about his practice and invited me along to mosque. Though I knew I was going to feel out of place among all those men, I went along to feel that I was doing the right thing for once in my life. I was there to hear about what Islam can offer me and why I should continue being a Muslim. I was looking to be convinced that this ritualistic community I had been co-opted into offered me more than just a group membership to be recognised as a believer.

When we arrived, we made salaah. I of course mimicked everything my brother did and moved my lips to what I thought was the rhythm of a prayer. After all that time, I still didn't know how to pray in the religion I was meant to love.

Men started filling up the mosque in droves, forcing us to keep shifting until there was hardly any space left between us. The air smelt of stale cotton clothing masked by the scent of attar.

When the Imam finally started his sermon, beads of sweat were just about to start rolling down my temples. He welcomed us with the most elaborate of Arabic greetings, which translates to 'May the peace, mercy and blessings of Allah be upon you.'

The sermon started with an anecdote about Good Friday. At first, I thought it was a logistics or safety announcement warning us to be vigilant in the shops when we were surrounded by so many people and vulnerable to opportunistic crimes. When the story finally wound down, I realised that the Imam was warning us against buying into the symbolism behind Good Friday. That we should not be corrupted and seduced into partaking in the rituals of eating the hot cross buns with its Christian symbolism. Somehow, he managed to make the bulk of the sermon about the warning while craftily weaving encouragement of holding onto our superior Islamic beliefs. Since I can remember, almost every secular trend has been interpreted as proof of the divinely predicted persecution of Islam. The mainstreaming of Christian rituals was also cause for protecting ourselves against the temptations of un-Islamic behaviour. I was amazed at how dedicated the congregation was to affirming the narrative being trotted out by the Imam. The creation of the 'other' was playing out in front of me. I looked around to check if I was the only one horrified by what I was hearing – and, to my disappointment, I seemed to be. I could not wait to get out of there.

That was the last time I set foot in a mosque. I had been let down too many times by walking in with hope and leaving with despair. Many people say that the followers' behaviour shouldn't be a reflection on the religion. Some say that Islam is a perfect religion, but its followers are imperfect. I disagree. The followers interpret, organise and deliver the religion, and it is therefore a product of their making. If a religion advises against misogyny, but its followers perpetuate misogyny in its name, then that is the religion. There is no amount of theoretical justice that can triumph over material injustice felt by living people in the name of religion. We do not live in theory. The teachings of a book cannot protect you simply by existing. If the practice of a religion is harmful, the religion is harmful. There was no amount of theoretical godly love that was going to protect me from homophobic, judgemental Muslims. The scripture that says do not judge others was not going to snatch out the tongues of people who called me a Waterslams. It does not work that way.

After experiencing what I saw as propaganda, I resolved to distance myself from the institution of Islam. The rituals, the meetings, the traditions and the rules. I believed I could maintain my connection with god without all the red tape of religion. It is what I was used to, but I had finally realised that there was no shame in not practising Islam. I reclaimed Waterslams to mean rebel rather than deviant. I was fine with being a Waterslams if it meant I didn't have to participate in the discrimination and judgement necessitated by my membership to the group. To me being a Waterslams now meant being a free thinker who could not be judged and ridiculed. I had nothing more to lose, since I was already on the outside, and if I ever felt like I made a mistake, I just needed to look back on all the things I had witnessed in the name of Islam.

When I was about eight years old, for instance, there was a young boy named Rodney who had come to join us at the mosque. He was probably 13 or 14. Rodney was a Coloured boy who was very clearly a descendant of indigenous Black people. He was exactly who Cape Malay and Indian Muslims would call a Boesman. I learnt that he was going to be initiated into Islam. The term they used was revert and not convert, because somewhere there was this bizarre belief that everyone is born Muslim and are just reverting back to their original path. That statement is generously laced with prejudice and superiority. The idea that Islam is the original state of humanity that everyone is born into immediately creates a hierarchy of humanity and makes religion something inherent in human beings. From that perspective, Rodney, who was to become Rashaad, was being cleansed of his misgivings to live the rest of his life in the righteousness and purity of Islam. I remember how clearly he was treated as an 'other' in our presence. It was almost reminiscent of the dismemberment of Sarah Baartman through the violence of the white gaze. Rodney was to be picked apart and put back to together for the glory of Allah. I suppose Rodney was looking for a home. After all, his family had abandoned him for an unknown reason, and he was in need of help. He was vulnerable to manipulation, and the mosque took full advantage of that to fulfil its evangelical obligations. Even then, it was all too horrific to me. I could not understand why Rodney wanted in on such a rigid, restrictive system. The truth is, he didn't. He just wanted help and the opportunity to grow in a sense of belonging.

I had always felt that subscribing to the practices and beliefs of Muslim people were not only incompatible with me, but also an indictment on my humanity. In many ways, I was grateful to my parents for not enforcing the rules on me. I was grateful that we were on the outside of Islamic circles. Although there would always be subtle jabs aimed at shepherding me back to the centre of Islam, I had no more appearances to keep up.

MY THIRD YEAR AT university was drawing to a close, and graduation time was upon me. I was finally getting my undergraduate degree. My father was actually present throughout the ceremony and visibly proud of me. All my father wanted was university graduates for children – and I was going to be the first one. It was not lost on me that his excitement was also driven by the fact that I was graduating with a BSc degree. I was pretty convinced his excitement would have been close to non-existent if it were a BA degree. He wanted science graduates for children, and I gave that to him. I chose a science degree to please my father – that was known. Since my dreams of studying drama were snubbed, I settled for the next best: becoming a clinical psychologist. I could have taken the BA psychology route and studied more creative subjects as I wanted to in the first place, but I did not, opting for hard science subjects and a BSc. This was largely for my father, so I was happy that he was present at the graduation.

The very colonial ceremony was long and uncomfortable, since the hall had no air-conditioning. The sounds of ululating mothers broke the dullness of a monotone voice butchering African and Arabic names. After two hours, the ceremony was done, and I started wading through the crowd to find my parents. I saw my mother's joyful face. My father was standing a few steps behind her. He was crying. My rough and tumble, sometimes terrorist drunkard of a father was crying tears – of joy? – for my achievement, without a drop of alcohol to cheer him on. I wondered how much of his tears were for the wasted seconds that stood between us. I don't think he expected to know what it was like to see his child graduate from university. Although his tendency to attach value to his children based on their academic achievements was warped, it meant a lot to him to see us succeed.

On the way to take my graduation photos, I got a call from the psychology department. They were calling to confirm that I had been offered a place in the honours programme. I could not contain my excitement.

I started screaming: 'Yes! Yes! Yes! Thank you! Thank you!'

In the next year I would be moving to Metanoia residence. At the time, it was the newest residence and the only one where men and women lived together, in single rooms. When I made the decision to apply for residence, I applied only for a place at Metanoia. I was not going to stay in a men's residence. The thought of having to share a room with anyone was unbearable, but even more so if it was going to be a hypermasculine, homophobic white man. The chances of finding myself in such a scenario were high under Stellenbosch's toxic, abusive residence culture. I wasn't prepared to take the chance.

My life was coming together as an adult. I had one degree to my name, and I was ready to fly from my parents' nest. I was nervous about being on my own, but I was ready to be an adult. I was going to come and go as I pleased with no questions or curfews. Most importantly, I was finally going to experience campus life with my friends. I couldn't wait to be a real student.

PART III
REVIVAL

Twelve

When I announced my decision to stay on campus to my parents, my mother was instantly resistant. She found every reason possible to suggest that I was not ready to go and live on my own. I had spent school holidays away from her for many years, but somehow leaving for residence felt too severe to her.

I was abandoning her, and there was nothing I could say that would convince her otherwise. We had always been allies under the tyranny of my father and, when the misery took the household down, we could always rely on each other for a soft place. My desire for independence felt like a betrayal of the unspoken pact we had made to always be there for each other. I promised her that I would be with her until her dying day, and here I was reneging on our agreement.

I could only think about myself and my needs at the time, but had I considered things from her perspective, it would probably have revealed a deep loneliness. My mother needed a companion. She was a very social person and found herself stuck, in love, with a complete social and emotional recluse. They had almost nothing in common except the desire to be in a relationship with each other.

My father had no appreciation for entertainment besides old TV shows. He had no interest in music. He seemed to be averse to fun in the popular sense of the word. He was everything my mother was not. He lived completely parallel to the life we lived. For that reason, naturally, my mother and I clung to each other.

I had to face my mother's dependency on me and the realisation that the person I looked to for sustenance was looking for it from me too. I felt the expectation placed on me was unfair, considering that I had given up so much of my adolescence to fill in the gaps my father left. I was ready to claim my youth before it was too late and inappropriate.

Though I considered undoing my decision to move out of the house, I had to choose my own happiness and allow my mother to reckon with her choice to marry and stay married to a man that was not all that she needed. If I appeased her one more time, I might never have regained control over my decisions. I could not live to quell my mother's disappointment. I had to go.

I arrived at residence during orientation week. Campus was an anthill. Seniors like me arrived after the first years had already settled in. They were practising for the annual rag, which involved building a float among other carnivalesque activities. These activities were compulsory and were generally signalled by the senior students on the house committee blaring music out of a speaker to wake first years up at the crack of dawn. A part of the reason I didn't want to stay in residence when I was a first year was to avoid residence culture. I had heard many stories about the toxic practices of university residences, especially men's residences. There was no reason for me to subject myself to more trauma than I had already become accustomed to. Voluntarily walking from one abusive hierarchy into another seemed like unnecessary self-flagellation. I skipped all these rituals in my first year and was entering on my own terms.

For the first time in my life, I was making decisions that centred on me and my needs. But it felt bad. I carried a guilt that was not mine to bear. I felt guilty for choosing to experience my youth as most of the peers around me did. Their parents offered them willingly to the world, but my mother had allocated my existence for everyday use.

Maybe somewhere in our blood the trauma of being owned endured to evolve into a parenting style. We cannot escape it, because if we bleed out, we die – and survival is all we know. As a people forced to live their lives as instruments, utilities, commodities, we learnt that human beings are ours to own, especially when they are made from us. As a people who never truly owned anything, knowing only dispossession and removal, we sought pride in the ability to create extensions of ourselves that we could claim forever. I think we are a people who have a deep collective need to be remembered in spite of how the power of the coloniser's pen washed us away. To witness yourself disappear from the description of wonder in the world is an indescribable cruelty. To know that somehow, somewhere you were more than the stories told about you but having no way to prove it makes for insecurity immeasurable. I have only been able to trace my mother's insecurities to her waking life. Her tendency to defend herself against any attempts to remove what she felt was hers was hereditary. The insecurity in my mother and her mother was not learnt behaviour unique to them. It was our colonial inheritance. She didn't want to be forgotten, again.

If I had the range of analytical depth to try and understand my mother in the context of the brutality visited upon her, I could have responded differently to her ownership of me. If I could see the bulldozers rumbling around in her mind every time something she cherished left her, I might have found more compassion for her.

But I too wanted my needs to be at the centre of consideration. I wanted to know what living without considering the consequences felt like. Though I would never fully experience that, I wanted to experience the luxury of worrying only about myself, even if that came at the expense of my close bond with my mother.

The initial shock of my move wore off quickly when my mother realised I was not disappearing from her life. My weekend visits gave us the chance to relive old times. I'm sure me being there gave her a sense of relief.

I never asked her, but I wondered what it was like having to face my father alone. My father was not a companion by any measure.

My mother had a childlike disposition through which she related to the world and me. The problem was that I was growing up and starting to lose the rose-tinted glasses. I was waking up to a world that my mother never had to live in. I was learning in a language she didn't speak and thought I knew things that she didn't. The elitism we internalise at university has a lasting impact on our core relationships at home.

My newfound acclaim as a university graduate cut me out and placed me above my mother. To me, she was a relic stuck in an era gone by, and I was the pinnacle of all enlightenment. There's a way in which knowledge is constructed within the academy that teaches us it is the *only* knowledge of value. It teaches us that the university language is the only intelligible form of communication. Perhaps my own need to be validated and recognised made me ripe for the picking, but I fell headfirst into a pit of self-congratulations.

I developed a quick tongue with a propensity for smart replies. My mother developed a resentment towards me and my increasing tendency towards correcting her. The power dynamic between Coloured parents and their children is something held in high esteem by adults. I remember Aunty Nisha once singlehandedly orchestrating the most unbearable chaos in her children's lives, and when she was told she was not entitled to do it without repercussions, she retorted, 'But I am the mother here! You can't tell me that!'

Our parents bought not only into the ownership of their children but also the power that came with it. Parenting itself is generally about power relations, and for many potential parents, the prospect of having a powerless being not only dependent on you but also subject to your whims and fancies can be pathologically seductive. Our reasons for wanting children are rarely interrogated, and when they are, they are rarely called by their names. For some, it is driven by a vanity embedded in the quest for replication of the self. We want to see who our children will look like and, in some cases, we try to engineer their looks through strategically chosen partners. For some of us, it's a silent co-optation into the eugenic project to maintain the purity of bloodlines and the mummification of family names. There are those who have children to fill voids of loneliness left by absent parents and disappointing lovers. Some of us try to please god and his decree to go forth and multiply. Even people who want to genuinely take care of and love children fail to be completely selfless in their ambitions, because the decision to love someone cannot be separated from the need to be loved in return. It has not been favourable to bring human beings into the world for a long time, if it has ever been. The decision to do so is rarely for the benefit of the child, and at its foundation is a power that seduces all those who don't question it. But our parents were often not the questioning type when it comes to matters supposedly of nature.

The tug of war between my mother and me would endure for years. Her need to feel affirmed as my guardian and, by implication, my superior vied to dominate my need for self-determination. I was discovering just how deeply enmeshed my mother and I were and how vastly different our once-mutual desires had become. All my life, my mother tended to my every need, shielding me from harm.

My choices in life were greatly shaped by her fears. I refrained from contact sports because she feared I would be injured the way my father was. Although he would never admit it, physical pain from an old shoulder injury sustained during a rugby match probably fuelled my father's need to numb himself with alcohol. I never questioned my preference for the arts and other non-physical forms of recreation, but internalising my mother's fears undoubtedly shaped my preferences and self-image. I was a mirror of her.

Though I had no desire to change who I was, I wanted to be myself outside of her supervision. That may be the best way to describe my mother's role in my becoming – she was supervising my evolution to check whether it mirrored her fears. I was, in many ways, her creation.

I was also a source of security for her. She feared that if I went too far from her, I would abscond on my obligation to take care of her after my father died, as she had planned. For her, the negotiation of this new prospect was complex.

The relationship between mother and son is a legendary subject. From Oedipus to Freud, the evidence of co-dependence between the two has been written down in history. My mother and I were the evidence, down to a tee. Unlike my mother, I would not submit to some prescribed destiny and accept life to be just the way it is. There was a life to be had, and I wanted it. She would often warn me about that thing called life and how it would humble me. But I was talking about a different life that she had not seen before. One of unconditional ease and abundance enabled by my hard work at university and my induction into the merit-based system as a credible authority on and producer of knowledge.

My dismissive way with her stemmed from a belief that she had no experience of the world that I was entering and would have none for the foreseeable future. In my mind, we were not the same.

I also struggled to accept her need for me to validate all her contributions and beliefs because she and my father had encouraged free thought among their children. That was the source of my feelings of betrayal. Why did they encourage all of this free thought and inspire ambitions of education if it were not to be used in their presence or even in response to them?

I would learn that my mother, in fact, knew the world I was entering. It was the same world that forced her to abandon her education at the age of 16. It was the same world that capped her potential at being a worker in a white-owned clothing boutique. It was the world that made becoming someone's wife the salvation she was hoping for. It was the world that denied her the bodily autonomy to make decisions about when and how to have children.

She knew it didn't matter how smart I was and how novel my ideas were, my position in the social hierarchy would always speak for me. The world she was talking about was the one all marginalised people experience. It was the world that defined me before I could introduce myself. Though she didn't have the language to help me decipher what she was trying to tell me, her warnings would come to make sense to me in later life. Ironically, through my mother, I learnt the importance of alternative language and knowledge, but also that everything I am learning has existed long before me – nothing is new. My father never spoke much, but his response to me was always, 'What you must still learn, I have already forgotten.' He was also not talking about what he learnt at school.

THERE WAS A PART OF MY world my mother would never experience and, to live in it, I had to escape her supervision. I had been in a psychological prison for as long as I could remember. Nobody around me could relate, nor would they ever learn to. I was a gay, questioning Coloured Muslim boy navigating one of the most notorious institutions of white supremacy in South Africa. I was locked out of desire for as long as I could remember. Reckoning with my sexuality had been a treacherous journey of shame and guilt long before the subtle rippling of my budding desires interrupted my childhood. Even before then, my access to the performance of desire was violently regulated by the stranglehold of heteronormativity. I have only known sexuality and desire as yearning. I have only wanted whatever lack was not. I wanted the opposite of fear – whatever that was. As a queer person, I never knew what I wanted, because what I was allowed to desire didn't fit me. What I saw around me was everything that was designed to kill me. It was less not knowing what I wanted and more imagining what I could want. Nobody around me could ever understand the world I was stumbling through – least of all my mother. No amount of support and guidance she had for me could help me navigate that part of my life. It was my burden and mine alone to bear.

I thought about it many times growing up. My mind was regularly consumed by a sad, miserable future. I could not imagine anything possibly joyous alongside a truthful existence as a queer person. My teen years were made up of ruminating over a shameful, lonely and despairing future. Growing up around the disdain for queer people I saw around me, not only in my family but also in the neighbourhood, at school and in popular culture, I resigned myself to an unhappy adulthood. I had been navigating and calculating my prospective life like someone vying for a prize in trigonometry. The lives of queer people are a calculation, if we are to survive. For those who don't care for survival, walking straight onto the train tracks and taking whatever may come becomes a life of endless sacrifice.

By my calculations, I had three options: to declare myself unattracted to anyone, sexually and romantically; to marry a woman and live in insufferable unhappiness while hoping death would visit sooner rather than later; or to spare myself the trouble and kill myself. None of the options I had considered had me anywhere near to the centre of consideration. All possibilities for living with my queerness put me at the mercy of other people's preferences. Except for death. That was about me.

Suicide is a complex entanglement of subversive, radical self-care and submission to society. We choose ourselves in the moment we decide to end lives of suffering and constant provocation. As queer people, we make ourselves unavailable for the constant disrespect and slow dying inflicted on us through sustained forms of gentle violence that leave us questioning our own sanity. We take back a power that we have been barred from exercising: the power over our bodies. We commit to a final act of love and the choice to love ourselves above the prescriptions of a world that teaches us an obligation to stay and be perpetually abused.

At the same time, taking our own queer lives pleases the system that is committed to annihilating us every day. Though the system would prefer to abuse and debase us on a daily basis, the goal is always to kill us. We are destined for death and erasure, and so taking our own queer lives is a service to the system too. Surviving motivates the system to try harder to kill us, while dying takes the job off its hands.

We do also exist beyond the constant violence of the system. We do also choose, in spite of the erosion of our agency. I was raised to understand that death by suicide is wrong by a god whose jealousy won't see him upstaged by the free will he created. Having lived under the power of the free will of other people, I see suicide as just another way that people die. There are many reasons why people choose to live, but very few can ever truly say they have reaped the rewards for it. Suicide is brave and honest in its message. It says that although everything, physically and socially, is set up to make me stay alive, I choose to die.

The bodily reflexes that pull us towards life, the societal shame attached to suicide, the guilt for leaving people who never cared enough behind in pain, the fear of eternal damnation for using a conditional free will – all of these structures that are set up to keep us alive were not enough for the person who died by suicide. Surely that is a grievous indictment on us as a society? People can and will choose when to end their lives and, for some, like queer people, it is the only choice they can ever truly make. Loving yourself does not always mean staying alive. Love does not always mean comfort and ease. Love is not what we think it is. Love does hurt us, maim us and – in its final form – kill us. When we truly reckon with the full spectrum of how love can be expressed, we may stop absolving it of its ugly faces. Perhaps it is for us to realise that death is not always, or perhaps ever, a bad thing.

Though I had unsubscribed from the formal structures of Islam, I still struggled to reconcile my queerness with my god, who was a Muslim, male god who hated queers. I had resolved to praise him on my own, but even outside of the structures I believed constrained me, god is still a homophobe. He is created in a book that endorses violence against me and he declares that endorsement to be his word. He is a proud homophobe. There is no power that constrains him to reconsider his hatred of me. He is free at my expense. It seemed foolish to believe in a god who created me to hate me.

I was trying to avoid a hell that was designed just for me. Even if I did everything I was supposed to do, I was still going to hell just for being who I am. This must be the height of psychosis. We are taught not to question god, but what happens when we are the contradictions that prove his questionable nature? Surely the Abrahamic, male god is the most chaotic, disorganised and error prone of them all. There was no way to reconcile myself with Islam, save for denying myself and my desires. I had to let it go too.

MY HONOURS YEAR WAS about letting go of the ties that were holding me back. I had a new life beckoning, and until then I had been committed to the ebb and flow of life. I had no power to challenge the structures that regulated me. But now I had to choose myself wholly or not at all.

My mother would always be my mother, but we would have to learn to exist anew. In some ways, we had to relearn how to have a relationship that was not based on inequality. She would have to make room for my agency to make decisions that didn't only centre on her needs, and I would have to develop a compassion for her that took into account that her life was not entirely of her own making. Not even our relationships as multiply oppressed people can escape the politics that define our lived experiences. There are no havens and safe spaces for us. If we are to survive, we do so through and within the political conditions imposed on us against our will. It is hard work to strive for functional relationships under conditions of marginality. I have since realised that I have never known what motherly love is separate from the politics of my marginalised identities.

In the end, my mother and I would have to make some agreements. She would have to accept that I am not a possession of hers and that my choices are not a reflection on her. I had to learn to understand her more and accommodate for her shortcomings. The process of learning and unlearning between us had many breakdowns and restarts, but with every setback I was always willing to try again. My mother and I have a lot of forgiveness between us. No matter how many betrayals we had experienced at each other's hands, there was always the sense that we wanted to be part of each other's lives. We are taught that we can't choose our family ties, but I believe we can. My mother and I have chosen each other over and over again. That is really the essence of relationships. We don't just exist alongside our relations but create them intentionally. Those that survive are the product of intention. We also choose those who are worth the time and energy it takes to keep rebuilding fallible relationships. Maybe to my mother there were no choices, but to me there are.

She would come to find comfort in Kahlil Gibran's poem 'On Children' to mourn the loss of my undivided attention. She came to me one day, unexpectedly, to share her awakening to my requests for autonomy and, although she would struggle for years to implement it practically, she shared her revelations. Probably the most difficult was her admission that, although I am her child, she cannot own me. That although I came through her, I did not come from her. I was now a part of the world, which also demanded my presence as much as I answered its call. Though it sounded horrific to admit, she had succumbed to expectations of owning me. I was her emotional backup plan.

For many parents of her generation, children were a reflection of them. Without the awareness to interrogate their own conditioning, that meant instilling the same thoughts and habits in their children. For my mother, the realisation that we were not one mind came too soon. The realisation never deterred her from trying to fuse our thoughts. Since I was a toddler she enjoyed regaling me with the most absurd fables about anything I observed in my natural environment. She enjoyed seeing my eyes bloom in disbelief as she held the sum of my knowledge about the world in the palm of her hand. As time went by and she became less of a source of information to me, the ritual failed to have the same effect. It was a loss she had to mourn, again. Her battle was to imagine me as connected to her, but not tied down with her. She was realising that leaving her could still mean loving her. That being away from her did not mean being without her.

This was her first step in letting me go.

Thirteen

On the first day of classes for my honours year, the February sun was ablaze. Stellenbosch was notoriously unbearable around that time of the year, but I was basking in my newfound autonomy. The sun was of little concern to me. In the first few days of orientation, I noticed a boy who had taken some third-year exams with me the previous year. He was one of the boldest queer people I had seen until then. He proudly and deliberately wore his queerness. He was small and skinny in stature and wore his hair in a gelled black mohawk. He read as Indian but was Coloured and went by the name of Neil Hassan. He wore flare jeans with an ornate leather belt that had a huge buckle in the shape of fanned playing cards. He represented everything I wished I could be. I would always steal glimpses of him and perhaps sometimes greet him when I saw him, because I didn't want him to see me gawking. His tiny frame radiated a revolutionary energy I had never before seen on queer people. I found that we generally walked with our heads bowed, simply grateful to be allowed. There were, of course, other queer people who expressed their queerness, but I had never seen someone who looked like me. His queerness was attached to a body that I could identify with and aspire to. For those reasons, he was both admirable and terrifying.

We were on the way down the stairs in the RW Wilcocks building after class when Neil asked me to wait for him. We cracked jokes about the lecture we had just had and decided where to go to wait for our next class. As we walked out of the building and turned into the honeysuckle-lined walkway, Neil threw a question my way.

'Have you ever had a boyfriend?'

I stopped dead in my tracks. There were so many thoughts to negotiate in that moment. I had been asked questions about my sexuality before, but they had always been geared towards questioning my lack of heterosexuality. Nobody had ever seen me enough not to shame me. He was not asking me if I was gay, he was telling me that he knew and was okay with it. In fact, it was not a factor. He wanted to know about my life or at least the life I should have. I had a choice to make; I could stay where I was and decline his invitation to meet him in unapologetic queerness, or I could break free from bondage. In that moment, all the possibilities I could not imagine for my life stood before me and, for the first time, I felt safe to take the risk of being myself.

I responded with an unaffected 'No'. The conversation delved into my life as a queer person and how we have had to navigate the pitfalls of a homophobic society. Neil came out to his mother when he was a teenager in a fundamentalist Christian family. I was in awe of the bravery and audacity to assert himself against such an oppressive institution, in the form of the religion and the family, while being so young. I took courage from his bravery, although I hated the fact that we lived in a society where being ourselves necessitated bravery. Nevertheless, I was encouraged by the possibility that I could choose life and possibly experience some happiness for it. I was not going to die. We walked back to Metanoia to hang out in my room and be as gay as we wanted before the next class. Neil didn't know it, but my life changed in his presence that day. He called me into my life with a simple question – and I heeded the call. I did not have to consider my parents, our neighbours, the extended family. Nothing else mattered, because finally I was validated in such a necessary way. I would never forget nor erase the contribution he made to my life. This was truly the freedom I was hoping for. I knew then that I had made the right decision to move away from home, although I would still have to live a double life for a while. Knowing what freedom was made it worth the effort.

I was not naive enough to think that I could open myself up to everyone. I still had to protect myself while getting to know myself as a queer person. I was finally meeting myself, and I was going to enjoy it all on my own.

Neil and I became inseparable. Whenever we appeared alone, people would wonder where the other one was. Even on the days when we didn't have classes, we would hang out together. I was probably more attached to him than he was to me, although I think he had not known genuine friendship until then. I became one of his only friends and provided unconditional friendship in its simplest form. He didn't have to pretend with me, and I wanted nothing from him but companionship. We were so comfortable with each other and shared every insignificant detail of our lives. Both of us were grateful to have found someone we could be honest with and not feel judged. We provided a safe space for each other. Neil was far more experienced with the ways of the world than I was, yet I think he found a sense of grounding with me and my old wisdom. In him I found a guide with which to explore the world and avoid the mistakes made by most.

Living on campus allowed me to release so many pent-up emotions and forms of expression. I had lived my life in fear of being uncovered by my femininity. The femininity that resided in the sway of my hips and the swing of my wrists seized up my joints like arthritis sent by patriarchy. The disdain we have for anything feminine, especially when it lives in bodies that read as male, has kept me locked into my body. I too internalised the shame of femininity and vehemently distanced myself from it. Though I tried to hide myself, I always yearned for the chance to express all parts of me without fear. When I finally admitted my sexuality to myself, I could express myself freely.

With Neil by my side, I had even more confidence to express myself and accept myself as I evolved. I explored make-up, letting my res mates put way too much mascara on my eyelashes one night. They were intrigued by how long my eyelashes were and – secretly – so was I. I wanted to enhance everything and become more of myself. At the centre of my desire was the need to be seen and acknowledged as a whole person. There was also another side to my expression: vanity. I became obsessed with perfection and beauty. Although I had always been very meticulous about my physical appearance, I wanted to project perfection. I enjoyed the attention it attracted, particularly because my face defied the gender binary. I wanted to express femininity, and I was finally being praised for it. When I went home on the weekends, I would steal my mother's foundation and lather it on my face before leaving. I would also line my eyes with her kohl and imagine I was Cleopatra before stepping out of the house. My relationship with the fear that oppressed me while growing up had changed. I wasn't as risk averse as I used to be, though I calculated all my actions for some guarantee of safety. I was comfortably living in two worlds. Sometimes separately and sometimes simultaneously. I was truly living and living truly.

WITH MY NEWFOUND QUEER FREEDOM, I started questioning many more rules I subscribed to – even the ones I imposed on myself. Since I was old enough to imagine a future, I vowed I would never drink. I vowed never to be my father. I had already noticed that some of my habits and ways resembled his and was convinced that I would be just like him if I drank. I was prepared to spend the rest of my life running from the pieces of my father that were alive in me. Since I stopped running from my queerness, I had to wonder what else I could have been missing out on. I started wondering if maybe I had been too harsh with myself, thinking I would turn into my father after taking alcohol. He was, after all, drinking to escape the world, while I had just found it. There was fun to be had and, although I abstained, I was always curious about what it would be like. I decided I would give it a try.

I tried drinking for the first time one night at the local Cubaña. I was there with friends from Metanoia, and they were excited, since it was unusual to them that I didn't drink. Stellenbosch holds quite a formidable reputation for its drinking culture among students, so I was an anomaly. When the waiter came, I ordered a cider to test the waters. It was sweet and slightly tart. I liked it. It tasted nothing like what I thought alcohol would taste like. It certainly didn't taste anything like the beer we were given as children to 'kill the worms'. I was pleasantly surprised. I also didn't instantly become obnoxious and sloppy as I expected. I could actually behave myself and walk out with all my friendships intact. I realised that my father's drinking was a very specific kind of numbing. He wanted to excise himself from the world, not enhance his experience of it. That's not what I wanted to do, so I would not become a version of him. It was not genetic nor destined. I was safe.

THE END OF THE FIRST semester of my honours year coincided with the start of my 21st birthday week. Neil and I decided that we would celebrate the entire week starting immediately after our final exam for the semester on the Monday night. We dressed up in our club outfits to write the exam. I aced that exam, and I knew it. When I left the exam hall, I had more than just my birthday to celebrate.

I had been to clubs before, but that night we were going to a gay club all the way in Greenpoint. I often look back and marvel at our spontaneity and how a distance of more than 40 kilometres seemed like nothing when there was fun to be had.

As we turned onto the N1 highway, I saw the twinkling city lights dancing at the foot of Table Mountain. They were just as excited to see me approaching as I was to be received by them. I had the same feeling I had as a child driving to Aunty Nisha's house at night. I was unaccustomed to thrill seeking so close to the carefully curated nightlife of the Cape Town CBD and Atlantic Seaboard. I had generally been confined to the familiarity of Edward Street in Tyger Valley and surrounds. It was the northern equivalent of aspirational nightlife activities, not too far from home. This outing felt not only more important but also more dangerous. My parents had no idea where I was or what I would encounter. I couldn't tell them, even if I wanted to, because I would not be able to explain my need to go to a gay club. I was completely on my own, except for having Neil with me. It was frightful and exhilarating.

Our destination was a club called Bronx, one of the oldest gay clubs in Cape Town, then apparently at its second location. When we walked in around 9pm, there were few patrons sitting forlornly with drinks in their hands. Nearly everyone turned around to look at us. We were probably the youngest people, which may have prompted the stares. I sat down at one of the high wooden tables close to the narrow door while Neil went to get us drinks. The club was dark and dingy, like a crack in a wall. It was not what I was expecting, but if that was what queer nightlife looked like, then who was I to argue?

We were in the gay village – a block of queer clubs mostly catering for white men and women. Although we occupied the space, it was evident that it was not made for us. At the time, I had no experience or understanding of the politics at play. To me, we were all queer and out to have fun in the comfort of our own community, which escaped all the -isms we lived through in the heterosexual world. Again, Neil was my buffer. I was oblivious to any of the politics around me.

As the night progressed, we moved deeper into the club. From the dancefloor you could see the bar right in the middle of the club, which was no bigger than a really big living room. There was a pole on the bar where daring patrons could attempt their stripper moves – without the stripping. Without me noticing Neil got up and jumped onto the pole. Instantly the room's attentions shifted to him. I looked and saw his tiny body swirling and gliding around the pole so much that I couldn't make out which parts were which. He looked as if he had been practising for years. I noticed that he was not asked to step down at any point the way gay men usually are in straight clubs. There they mostly want women on elevated surfaces expressing their sexuality for the multiplied male gaze observing from below. The space was for us as a community, although straight women also enjoyed the courtesy.

When he got off the bar, he returned to the table where I was sitting with an acquaintance of his. He knew him from the club scene. He had the cutest, youthful face framed by the woolly curls the Bible described Jesus to have. He was shy and somewhat unsure of why he was there. After observing him and Neil for a while, I realised he was brought there for me. Neil had organised me a companion for the evening. I had never had any romantic interactions with anyone in my life before, casually or seriously. I had never even kissed anyone. The thought was scary and exciting at the same time. The multiple bottles of Smirnoff Spin had already washed away my sense of caution. The boy signalled for me to follow him to the restroom. I looked over at Neil, for guidance. He gave me a mischievous smile that let me know I was safe. I followed, but Neil's friend was already out of sight. The toilets were even darker and dingier than the club. The smell of urine and mothballs should have made me turn around, but I was determined to continue. I couldn't tell if it was because I had had too much to drink or because I wasn't wearing my glasses, but I could hardly see a thing in front of me. I took a few more steps towards the sink and saw a silhouette that matched his frame. I mumbled something, and he responded. He came closer to where I was standing in the middle of the restroom where I was already preparing myself to be kissed. My eyes were closed, partly in anticipation of the kiss, and partly because of the weight of drunken euphoria. I leaned forward, stumbled and – in an attempt to regain my footing – I opened my eyes. I was alone in the restroom, wondering if I had followed an apparition. I couldn't tell if the kiss happened either, even if it was just a swift brush past my lips. I was embarrassed. I walked back to where Neil was sitting, disappointed at being rejected.

Until today I still can't figure out if that was my first kiss. Not that it matters much, but it is telling of the circumstances under which queer people have to experience romance. In many ways, romance for us is an apparition appearing and disappearing at will. Throughout our lives, we remain unsure if we've experienced romance – and often love – because it is often done in hiding. Ours is an exiled romance, constrained by the harsh judgement of the sunlight in which bigotry flourishes. We look back on our relationships and wonder if we were ever loved. What does love and romance look like in the dark? Can we see all its curves and cracks the way those who walk freely in the light can? How do we recognise something we cannot see fully under the dim blue light of the moon? Our sight is obstructed by strobes in underground universes made for us as safe spaces. The privilege of failing in the daylight can never be underestimated when someone like me still wonders what a first kiss feels like. By university age, most people have already experienced at least one teenage love affair, which probably signalled the end of the world when it died, with parents and siblings to offer comfort in fully lit rooms. We don't love in the light, we don't fail in the light, we don't win in the light, and we don't live in the light unless we force ourselves into it. Even today, it is a job to be visible as a queer person. Nothing is organic.

When we left the club, the sun was already rising. Despite being disappointed I was ecstatic to have completed my gay rite of passage. I forgot about the boy as quickly as I met him – after all, my freedom was not located in pretty boys, and I was out to have a good time.

I had to attend a meeting with my supervisor on campus later that morning, so we had to get back to Stellenbosch. On the way, we stopped at Neil's family home in Goodwood for something to eat. Nothing could have prepared me for what I was about to encounter, even though Neil softly mentioned that his mother wasn't wholly accepting of him. It was around 7am when we arrived, and the house was quiet. I was slightly anxious, not knowing what to expect since I had never met an elder of my community on the assumption that my sexuality was known. His mother was a small woman, with neatly parted short hair. She was simply dressed, in a long-sleeved vest, tracksuit paints and slippers. Like most Coloured mothers, she was already cleaning the house. She welcomed me warmly with a visible curiosity. She spoke to Neil with a sustained passive aggression, lamenting his failure to fulfil some or other obligation. They tugged at each other with a friendly hostility that I had never seen before. I wasn't sure if it was based on a warped humour that only they understood or if it was just toned down for my convenience. Whatever it was, it was uncomfortable.

She then turned her attention to me, to interview me about my studies and my family while Neil was preparing breakfast for us. Her questions were rooted in genuine interest and concern for me and my life. This was new to me. I had always anticipated outright rejection based on my sexuality, especially from elders. I could not imagine scenarios in which I would still be addressed as a person of interest. I was pleasantly bewildered by it all but, like a child, I allowed myself to be guided by Neil's energy. He was used to it and understood his mother's intentions better than I did. We ate our breakfast while Neil and his mother continued their passive-aggressive dance. When we finished, it was around 9am, and we had to make our way to Stellenbosch for my meeting.

'When are you two going to get girlfriends?' Aunty Marilyn asked as we were on our way out. 'You must like women, like the Bible says.'

I was completely thrown off balance by this sudden aggressive evangelism. Neil brushed it off and hurried us out of the house. I would have many more similar interactions with her, but we came to accept each other.

Aunty Marylin was preparation for what awaited me when I would come out to my parents. I anticipated an uphill battle. I wondered about Neil and how he coped with all the microaggressions, which I would learn were not only handed out by his mother. He had developed a thick skin for survival, but somewhere it must have hurt. I understood that she too was living through her own process of reckoning in a world that taught her, like it taught my mother, what an acceptable life looks like. The damage done to us, their children, however, arose out of an inability to invite us into their journeys as we embarked on our own.

Queer people often make many personal sacrifices to retain proximity to family. Somehow, we always seem to be required to accept the subtle and sometimes overt violence of religious heteronormativity. When we retaliate, we are the aggressors. Under any circumstance of power imbalance, one will always find the truth when inverting the order of things. Those on the losing end of society's (in)justice never enact violence outside of violence being visited upon them first. I don't take issue with our parents for being proxies for social violence. They are doing what they understand to be expected of them. They too are protecting themselves from a ridicule they know so well.

But I do take issue with their inability to see our humanity. Knowing what harm awaits them in the world, parents should create a safe space for their children. And they do more often than not, but the safeness of our family homes is often revealed to be conditional when we dare to choose ourselves over the aspirations of our parents. They cannot cop out of humanity that easily. If their gods require worship through violence against their own children, they must find new gods. Love for queer people cannot have a limit. There can be no limits to how many changing parts of them are acceptable.

I arrived at my meeting with a few minutes to spare. My clothing reeked of smoke, and my fading make-up told the story of where I had been. My beard had started making its way back, like a growing plant seeking out the sunlight. My supervisor was Anthea Lesch, who was one of a few Coloured women in psychology at Stellenbosch. When I first encountered her in my third year, I was instantly drawn to her. For the first time in my academic career, I felt represented and seen by someone. I felt like I was being taught by someone who showed up for me. She was not only there to earn a salary but to bring the next generation of graduates like her forward. We were both from Kraaifontein, and we discovered that one of my classmates throughout primary and high school was her cousin. It was as if we were always connected. I didn't hesitate to choose her as my supervisor when the opportunity came.

She opened the door with a warm smile and welcomed me into her office. I was slightly shy about arriving in the previous day's clothes, visibly still covered in the dancing spirits of the queer ancestors guiding me. She took no obvious notice of it, but throughout I wondered what she was thinking. I was also changing from the reserved, restricted student she had known. To me, expressions of my queerness still clashed with values of collegiate professionalism, which I believed I had to present to figures of authority. Although she was cool, not only as a supervisor but also as a person, I still felt like I had let her down. I was navigating a new guilt for defying the conventions that tried to erase my queerness. Queerness is not only about sexuality but also the scope of our lives and the agency to live as we choose. I was struggling to reconcile that I was still worthy of consideration and respect, even if I present myself physically in a way that the establishment doesn't endorse.

Anthea gave me a knowing smile that I felt not only acknowledged but also validated me. She would never ask me about my evolution, knowing it would make me uncomfortable, but always knew to communicate to me that I am safe to be who I choose to be in her presence. She accepted that I was the narrator of my own story, and her job was to hear what I presented. I appreciated the opportunity to breathe easily.

Fourteen

I opted for a house party for my 21st birthday. Parties in the house had a heavy meaning to me, but I too wanted my turn like everyone else. I asked my parents to leave the house to me for the weekend. They obliged and booked a little seaside retreat in Sea Point. I knew I was not prepared to tone myself down for anyone at the biggest celebration of my life, and we were not the kind of family who made a fuss about birthdays – not even 21sts. For once our lack of connection both at home and with our extended family worked in my favour.

I asked my mother to cook a big pot of lamb curry and got my friend Lauren to make a lasagne. I chose food that would go far to make sure we had enough on a small budget. Tayshira got a friend to make me a chocolate Bundt cake, and Dominic's aunt made a huge batch of koesiestes. It was a humble spread, but we would all eat. I had invited some high-school friends, my cousins Keinin and Reagan, Neil and some of his friends. I had an intimate affair planned with only people that were close to me and a few acquaintances for ambience. I was so busy preparing and arranging things that I didn't even change into something fancy before the guests arrived. I stayed in my slippers throughout and wrapped an embroidered pashmina around my shoulders to complete the look.

By the time Neil arrived, the party had already started, but we were waiting for him to start singing happy birthday to me. He arrived with a gift that he wanted me to open immediately. I could not have anticipated what I found: a huge dildo with a suction-cup end. The party was officially in full swing as everyone broke into an off-key, unsynchronised rendition of 'Happy Birthday'.

I was unaware of what was happening in the kitchen until I heard the loud whirring of a blender. I looked over to see Neil holding my mother's blender, which contained a pinkish-brown sludge purported to be a birthday drink for me, made up of every type of alcohol in the house. Drinkers have an odd obsession with seeing each other completely wiped out, and the fun for everyone was the possibility of that happening to me. My drink was poured into the biggest beer mug in the house – a souvenir from one of my father's trips to Germany. As they brought the drink to me, everyone started chanting some drunken instruction meant to encourage me to drink it in one go. I obliged without spilling a drop. The rest of the night played out mostly at the dining room table where we had loud, unhinged conversations, played card games, ate and drank some more.

At some point someone put the dildo in the middle of the cake, where it stayed for the rest of the night, acting as both a prop for photos and an enhancement. I was sitting at the head of my father's dining room table, fully present as a queer person. Everyone in the house knew that I was queer and were happy to be there with me. I was at an unprecedented level of freedom and acceptance. I didn't experience it as such at the time because I was living through it, but I would always look back on that evening with wonder for making it to a place I never thought I would reach in life. As it proceeded, the night started becoming a blur to me. People left, while some decided to stay over. I became more and more energetic. I was dancing, almost hysterically, while everyone else slept. I could not stop myself. I was in a trance where only the music and I existed. I must have danced myself to sleep that night because I woke up on the lounge floor. It truly was the best 21st I could have asked for, because there were no rules. Years later, Neil told me that someone put ecstasy in my birthday drink, which could explain why I was on such a hysterical high, although I had taken it voluntarily in Bronx in the week leading up to my birthday and hardly reacted to it at all.

I didn't know how to feel about Neil's revelation, especially since it could have gone very wrong, but I guess that is the dark side of liberation and exploration. I had to console myself with the fact that I had survived to tell the tale, but that violation of my consent left me feeling conflicted about my experience of the evening.

My party was only meant to last for one night, but having the house to ourselves for the whole weekend seemed like such a waste if we didn't make the most of it. On the Saturday morning, those of us who stayed behind cleaned the house to prepare for the second day of festivities. I had no idea what a hangover felt like. I could drink the night away and wake up as if nothing happened. No headaches, no lethargy. I was like a battery powered toy, always ready to be wound up. Close to sunset we were ready for another party. We resolved to make a potjie, allowing us minimal effort in the kitchen and more time enjoying the party. Neil invited his cousin Leroy and his friends around. Lauren's boyfriend, who was also a friend of Tayshira and Dominic, arrived with some of his friends too, so the house was even fuller than the night of the actual party. We stood around the fire, smoking weed and drinking. I had never been so happy in my life.

Besides the obvious laughter emanating from cracking jokes and the abandon of prime youth, I was undergoing an evolution. I was among people I loved and felt no need to hide. I was not being questioned or ridiculed. Again, a place that only existed in my imagination was breathing all around me. The evening floated seamlessly from one mood into the next. The night had a more contained euphoria to it than the previous one. By the end of the night, Keinin, Reagan and I were the only ones left and had the mammoth task of cleaning and restoring the house to its former clinical glory. The dining room table was fully covered with empty bottles and ashtrays. The kitchen was filled with dishes and glasses. Keinin and I could barely stand, but somehow the thought of my father's wrath when he saw the house in that state propelled us to give cleaning up our best efforts. We cleaned the house so meticulously that anyone walking in after us would never have known a party happened there.

To reward ourselves for our sterling efforts, we sat down at the counter, where so many drunk people had sat before, to have one more drink together. My vision was blurry, and my voice sounded as if it was coming from somewhere outside my body. I was swaying side to side and mumbling incoherent thoughts out loud. When I finally heard myself, I was so alarmed by my own lack of control that I slid off the chair to go to bed. I was content and happy as I drifted away to sleep. I was home for the holidays.

A MONTH LATER, TAYSHIRA and Dominic, married by now, came to visit. Their arrival in Cape Town was always met with excitement as is customary for the 'prodigal' children who left the hometown to pursue wealth elsewhere. They had by that time managed to build a respectable life in Johannesburg, and I, for one, admired them.

I was out with Neil almost every night of the week and went home to greet them shortly after they arrived.

'How was your 21st?' Dominic asked me with a knowing smile, almost inviting me to spill the beans. 'Jy't wee angegaan, nè girl?'

He was alluding to something. I acted like I didn't know what he meant.

'I heard from Vinny and them it was a wild party.'

When he said that I realised that he knew and was inviting me to come out to him.

'Yah, it was fun,' I said, still cautious.

'Have you told Mom and Dad yet?'

'No, but I will.'

'You must tell them. We mustn't have secrets in the family. It will be fine.'

Tayshira was standing around listening to us. Someone called Dominic away, leaving us alone for a minute.

'So, what do you think? How do you feel?'

I couldn't yet recognise the ridiculousness of asking my cisgender, heterosexual sister how she felt about my sexuality. I was more concerned about how she felt about me. She gave me an uncomfortable smile, belaboured with reservation and said, 'It's alright.'

That is all the person I nearly idolised had to say about one of the most important journeys in my life. I accepted it and moved on. But I could sense a palpable discomfort in her for the duration of their stay. She was contemplating how my newfound agency impacted on her place in our relationship. My claim to a sense of control over myself meant that her role in my life had to be renegotiated to restore the previous power imbalance my uncertainty afforded. Our relationship had always depended on a power imbalance that she was on the upper end of. I didn't see it as such at the time, but her lukewarm response was a red flag. I paid it no mind.

On the night of their return to Johannesburg, I was having pre-club drinks with Neil at Spur when I got a text message from my mother: 'I've been told that you are gay. Is it true? I won't be angry, just tell me.'

My heart sank. Dominic had taken it upon himself to tell my mother after I had expressly told him I had not done it yet. I was outed before I was ready, but there was nothing I could do. I was surprised but somewhat relieved that I didn't have to initiate the conversation. Her welcoming tone helped. I knew she would understand. It was my father I was afraid of.

I responded: 'Yes, Mom, it's true. We'll talk when I get home.'

We ended up not going to the club, and I headed home around 1am. I walked into the house quietly, making sure not to disturb anyone. I took my shoes off and sat on my bed for a minute. I was grateful that my mother didn't reject me and gave me a safe space to confide in her.

But then my bedroom door swung open with the force of the Southeaster. It was my mother with a scowling expression on her face.

'Where do you come from now?'

'From Neil, Mommy.'

'I will never accept this!' she screamed in a whisper.

'What do you want from me, Mommy?'

'I know this is a biological thing, but I will never accept it! Never!'

'Mommy, just leave please.'

'And I'm telling your father in the morning.'

My heart shattered. My own mother ensnared me, so that she could humiliate me. I was scared and disappointed. Mostly disappointed in myself for trusting that she would support me. All my life I was afraid that my family would turn on me, and when the time came to truly watch my step, I succumbed to warm, fuzzy feelings of family. Family that was never there in the first place. The weight of what had just happened was unbearable. I changed into my pyjamas, turned off the light and went to sleep hoping I wouldn't wake up.

When I did, none of the weight of my impending humiliation had dissipated. I sat in my bed trying to work out a plan to sneak out of the house without being noticed. I had to – at all costs – avoid seeing my parents. I sneaked past their bedroom to the bathroom to shower. Everything was in slow motion and on fast forward at the same time. I was a hostage in my own home, trying to plan an escape. I managed to get back to my room unseen, although they could hear me moving around in the house. I had butterflies in the pit of my stomach. I was preparing to be exiled from home. I just knew it was over for me. The previous few months of reckoning helped me come to terms with the possibility of having to live without my parents. I was somewhat prepared to go out on my own. I still had my residence room for the rest of the year, so I would be fine. I had calculated a few possibilities in my head. I was going to be fine, but no amount of preparation could calm the fear that had overcome me. Whatever my fate, I had to get out of that house immediately.

I moved stealthily towards the door, turned the handle slowly and turned it back to its default position, so that it didn't make a sound. I saw that my parents' bedroom door was open, and nobody was in the kitchen. That meant they could only be in the lounge. I had to take the chance and hope that they didn't want to see or speak to me. As I approached the front door, my father's voice gently apprehended me, 'Jamil, come here.'

'Fuck!' I mumbled under my breath. I couldn't escape the chiding I was sure was about to follow. I turned back and approached the couch. My father looked as if someone had knocked his breath out of him. He looked tender and hurt. There were no signs of anger or rage anywhere in him. My mother, on the other hand, looked like a dragon ready to incinerate me. She was livid. She showed me – clearly – there was no chance for redemption.

'Your mother has told me that you're gay. Is it true? I want to hear it from you.'

'Yes, it is true.'

'I need to understand what this means ... Do you want to be a woman?'

'No, Dad. I am a man. I'm happy with being a man, I am just attracted to other men.'

'Okay, so you're not going to walk down the road in women's clothing?

'No.'

'Who is that boy Neil you're always with? Are you an item?'

'No, he's just a friend.'

The questions kept coming. My mother was still huffing and puffing next to him, but we were having a conversation. My father genuinely wanted to understand what my sexuality meant. He needed to understand the difference between a gay man, a drag queen and a transgender person. I had never felt so cared for by my father in my life. I felt like he was protecting me from my mother. He concluded that my sexuality was caused by a physiological hormonal imbalance, and he was sympathetic to it. Both my parents were concerned about what the people would say and how I would conduct myself in public. I stopped the agony.

'Being gay does not mean I want to be a woman. I've always been gay. You've always had a gay son. Nothing has changed, except the knowledge that you now have. I have been in agony for the last 20 years. I am now the happiest I have ever been, and for that you should be happy. I understand that this affects you, but with all due respect, it is not about you. Don't put me at the mercy of the people, because when you lost your job and needed help, the people were nowhere to be found. I am just me.'

My dad nodded. My mother seemed to have calmed down somewhat. I left the house beaming with pride for how I handled myself. I didn't have to fight. My parents did not disown me. My worst fear had passed me over, and I was still alive. There was nothing that could shake me after that. I could not believe the person who had caused me so much relentless grief became the one to create a safe space for me to come into myself. It remains a difficult thing to reconcile, but I have learnt that one must always leave room for people to become who they are, be it good or bad.

My grandfather's words ring in my head, in all their simplicity: 'Jy is nooit te sleg om goed te raakie, en jy is nooit te goed om sleg te raakie.' He was talking about the acceptance of human beings as infinitely wonderful and infinitely flawed at the same time. I have learnt to live in harmony with contradiction. To this day, my father's choice to pull me closer and understand a foreign part of me that he had never encountered remains one of the most meaningful events in my life. He loved me with the sensibilities of a rickety old sewing machine: broken, but still trying to stitch something together.

Fifteen

A few months earlier I had been cleaning the car and rummaging through loose papers in the cubbyhole. I found a letter from the bank addressed to my father. It was a credit card statement in his name, showing that he was indebted for R40 000. I shrank. My mother and I had watched him make hardly any adjustments to his spending habits after he left Rudolf Chemicals, while we all knew his salary was not guaranteed. We had asked him multiple times if we could afford the life we were living, and he had told us to mind our own business.

We had recently sold the Mercedes because it was too old and expensive to maintain, but my father's affliction with escapism did not only drive him to seek comfort in a whisky bottle. He also self-soothed with spending money. His weakness was groceries. At any given time, our grocery cupboards looked like a to-scale model of a supermarket aisle. Everything stocked in multiples. After a while, he developed delusions about the attention the cashiers were fixing on him whenever he checked out his purchases. When he came home, he would tell my mother: 'Daai cashier kannie gegloe 'et ek het soe baie goed gekoepie! Hulle praat sieke nou nog onne mekaa!' He didn't have an addiction to self-gratification but got high off spending on us and the household. He was chasing the feeling of accomplishment that came with providing for his family, so maybe that was still self-gratifying.

He was, however, chasing it away. The need was so strong that he failed to heed any warnings about irresponsible spending and debt. We had been living in the house for 22 years by that time, and my father still had not managed to pay the house off. Two years before, he had called Tayshira up to ask her to take ownership of the house, because he would not be able to square up the debt by the end of the 20-year bond agreement. Instead of shrinking, the debt on the bond had grown over the years because my father was accessing the money in the bond. We had been living on revolving credit all that time. In reality, we were a working-class family living a middle-class lifestyle. Tayshira agreed and took ownership of the house. The point of the agreement was to secure the house for my mother after my father died, and he would still pay the bond instalments to her. It was a way to extend the time on the bond agreement. He was trying to keep his promise as a provider not only of resources but of security.

When Tayshira announced that she was selling the house, we were devastated. She needed to free her name of debt and decided to let the house go. With it, my mother's life-long dream of having her own home went up in flames. It was her insecure childhood returning to taunt her. She would have to move, again.

My own dream was always to inherit the house from my father. I thought inheritance was everyone's birth right. I had known no other home. All of our memories clung to the walls of that house. That house was already committed to a future I had imagined myself into. It was meant to carry me into that future. It was given a life and a job it hadn't agreed to. In the 22 years we lived there, we had threatened at least once a month to break it apart. It witnessed all the times my parents charged me with the responsibility to preside over their many would-be divorces. We were so often unhappy there, and no amount of security could truly soothe us. Our home, like my queerness, was something that still needed to be achieved. We aspired to have a home, and the house became the waiting room in which we were trying to figure it all out.

I've often looked back and wondered if we really lost anything by losing that house when we had not managed to make it much of a home in 22 years. Maybe the house knew we were not fully present within it and decided to let us go. Whatever it was or was not, there was a certain sadness that settled with the announcement.

I wasn't particularly saddened by the reality of having to leave our home, but my mother ... I was shattered for my mother. Every single affliction she bled onto her family could be traced back to her insecurity about having a home of her own. It had taken many years and many fights to understand this. After every emotional setback and breakdown at the hands of my emotionally absent father, her comfort came from knowing that she had a permanent place of residence. At times, it was the only thing she could console herself with. For her, a world was ending. A refuge was crumbling, and like the force of annual summer floods in Gauteng, there was nothing she could do to stop it.

Insecurity had once again found her and reminded her that for people like us security is an illusion powered by generational land dispossession. I had the time to make myself a new dream, but my mother was swallowed whole. She was angry, and she wanted to blame someone. She blamed Tayshira for not caring enough. She blamed my father for not doing enough. She probably blamed herself for not planning enough.

The truth was that the odds were always stacked against us. We were positioned as the collateral damage in the class war that makes white people richer and Black people poorer. For us, the access to resources kept transforming as many times as we were willing to transform, but the catch was that we were stuck in a constant loop of starting over and trying again. It was the aspiration to truly justify our status as the better Coloureds that kept us trying. There is nothing worse than a disgraced arrogance. In that way, although rooted in prejudice and inequality, we were also trying to attain full humanity, however false. A false humanity premised on the separation from the humanity of other Coloured people and, worse still, the further separation from the humanity of other Black people could never find rest. We would have to keep proving the same thing over and over – an anxiety-provoking existence.

On the day we moved the last things out of the house, I was on campus. I had not been involved in the process of moving because I was focusing on the last stretch of academics for the year. It was the conclusion of both my second degree and the home I had known for 21 years. My parents sold most of their furniture and homeware, leaving only beds and clothing to be moved. Technically I had already moved out of the house, so the ceremony held little significance for me. I didn't say goodbye to any of our neighbours either. We were not only moving out but also moving on. Our move was also tinged with shame for not being able to maintain the façade we put up for so many years. I just didn't care to face any of it. We thought we were special, we fucked it up – and that was all there was to it. I was ready to be emancipated from the charade too. It had been years of airs, graces and pretence. It was exhausting and constraining. I was also not prepared to present a former version of myself for anyone's comfort. I was ready for life to be about me, unconditionally. It was done.

After the move, I woke up one morning with a heaviness I recall vividly. My actions were dictated by time and necessity, not desire. I wanted to lie in bed all day, but my mom was coming to fetch me, and I had to get ready. I got up to make my bed, and as I gripped the duvet to shake it the first time, my heart jumped into my throat. I ignored it. I lifted the duvet for the second time, and my knees dislodged. I let the duvet go and sat down on the bed, staring at the door for a few seconds. My eyes were wide and still. A loud guttural cry stormed out of me. I was surprised. I didn't know why I was crying, but it felt so good. I was crying for all the times I had had to be strong. I was crying for my mother's worst nightmare coming to fetch her again. I was crying for not being able to stop my father's recklessness. I was crying for the years I spent in bondage and hiding. It was the release of so many foreign realities forced on me and the chance to live anew. The loss I mourned was a rebirth for me. I had begged and pleaded with a deaf and mute god for all those years to release me from shame, and finally I had released myself. I was the god I sought, finally free.

Truthfully, I didn't really want that house. It came with too much baggage that I didn't have the space for. I suppose it could have helped to start a life with more security, but my life was never going to be the one those systems cared to secure. I realised that when I came into myself, and although I had not yet seen the life I wanted, I knew it existed outside and alongside the structures that constructed me until then. My queer life was yet to be revealed to me. It did not yet exist, and I was not going to find it in the place where deprivation reigned. Moving away presented me with an opportunity to create a life rather than to inherit one.

Security, too, can be a noose. I was always taught to want security neatly packaged into a predictable trajectory. I was to go to university, study a prestigious science degree, get a job in the field I studied, work my way to the top and accumulate assets. I was always eager to attain it too, but queer lives are not that easily pacified. There would always be the yearning for something else, something more. What to many is a curse is to me a blessing. What to others means freedom, to me means imprisonment. I was relieved of the expectations so many who came before me had internalised. A fluid life with space for negotiation opened up for me. It was a space to fail and learn without toppling an entire house of cards built on the potential others saw in me. There were no more traditions and cultures I needed to accept and abide by since my very existence challenged them to re-evaluate their own humanity, under duress. I was released of a jealous, bloodthirsty god and his pack of hyenas always nipping at my ankles.

We lost a house, but I gained a world. Though I would still revisit it many times in my mind, I was never going back there or anywhere where rules come before personhood. I was going anywhere and everywhere but there. It was the start of my unknowing, unlearning and undoing. I have left parts of me in every place I've been since because I learnt that home is not a destination but a journey to finding a place where we can just be ourselves.

Epilogue

It has been nearly ten years since I commenced my journey into personhood and its many winding turns. I say personhood, because for me the journey centred intersectionality in its way of reconciling multiple positionalities, both privileged and oppressed. I have also embodied my queerness in ever-evolving ways, realising that coming out is not an event when it does happen, and that queerness is no less valid in its absence.

In April of 2011, nine months after we moved out of our home, I met Jason van Leeve at Lauren's house over Easter Weekend. It was the first time I had felt completely safe in the company of a cisgender heterosexual-presenting man. It was as if my then unapologetic queerness attracted his humanity to me. Indeed, he was the epitome of humanity and became one of my best friends.

The night we met, we had a conversation about sexuality and its spectrum of experience. When asked the question: 'Could you ever see yourself in love with another man?' Jason responded, with absolute ease: 'I promised myself that I would allow myself to experience everything at least once.' I knew in that moment that this was someone I could allow into my life. He was one of the first men, unrelated to me, who saw me as human and was genuinely interested in me beyond the sensational accessorising of gay men. He didn't seek entertainment of me, nor did he wish to turn me into a commodity.

I became a part of his family, and our relationship grew. Jason was probably my first love. I loved him as more than a friend. We had a romantic relationship based solely on emotional attraction. I also simultaneously developed a wonderful friendship with his wife, Shumonay, which endures to this day. She was completely comfortable with our love and respected our relationship, knowing that we both loved and respected her too. I have learnt since then that the spectrum of emotional life within queerness is vast. Queer love is made up of beautiful things that transcend the binaries we are socialised into. I was very privileged to be able to share space with someone who didn't pathologise my love. Though it should be common, it is not. It is often not possible to escape the violence of the normative, gendered gaze that constantly tries to squeeze us out of sight.

Jason left us in 2019. I mourn his absence in multiple ways, but mostly I celebrate the life that gave mine so much. Through our love, I learnt that I never had to accept a lesser place in society, even though I am scared of the repercussions. I honour our love with this story. He always enjoyed my style of storytelling when we would smoke weed in his garage and end up in two respective balls of laughter on the floor. This book is an ode to queer stories that never see the light of day. It is the limitlessness of queerness that scares people because it brings so sharply into focus the inadequacies of normative lives.

Throughout my life I have found that I have come out multiple times. As my understandings of sexuality and gender evolved, so did my expression of it. Presumably heterosexual in nature, the premise of coming out is violent in its requirement only of queer people to confess themselves to the world. It is the initial coming out that tends to create a pattern of continuous confession for the comfort of normative society. Queerness is expected to issue a warning, alerting everyone to where the emergency exits are located, if it is to be allowed into the room. We must almost always give heterosexual people the option to be spared the displeasure of our presence.

I tend to believe that the decision to confess myself cultivated an expectation that I would always announce the ways in which I have changed throughout my life. The purpose of such confession was never for my own happiness, but to give those around me a way to prepare for how to treat me. It has never been enough for me to just be, hence I liken the journey of being with that of finding home – a place where one can simply be. If I had known better, I would not have made my coming out an event, although in my case it was decided for me. I have only just come to a place where I can be without qualifying my existence. I have always wanted an audience to hear the exchange I had with my parents, because I think it is an important moment to witness an assertion of queerness that decentres heterosexual concerns. We have the agency to choose, and the evolution of queer experiences are too dynamic to be subjected to repeated coming out. We must, in spite of the symbolic and physical violence meted out to us daily, live without justification.

Heteronormativity is insidious and ubiquitous. I have endured two relationships in which I was playing into gender roles. I have found myself emulating my mother, the loyal and dutiful wife, to appease the egos of gay men who embodied their masculinity in the same toxic ways that we critique heterosexual men for. We are unfortunately still in search of lives free from the bondage of binaries, but while we are searching we must be aware of the ways in which we replicate the oppression we resist. There is no one way to be queer or to love queerly, and the submission to binaries is a betrayal of the vastness of queer life.

There are those who will ask why, if queer people choose to submit to binaries, it cannot be respected as agency. We can respect people's agency while also acknowledging their participation in maintaining unequal power relations. Traditional gender relations, regardless of the bodies that perform them, are inherently unequal, and inequality is a betrayal of queerness. The Cuban-American academic José Muñoz reminded us that queerness is the future – a boundless future without all the trappings of the world we currently inhabit. Declining participation in restrictive, oppressive practices will secure a queer future that serves everyone's interests of freedom.

It was within one of these relationships that I finally found cause to excise religion from my life completely. Though I had stopped partaking in the rituals of religion, it would take time for me to completely distance myself from it. In 2014 I went to New York for two-and-a-half months to help a friend organise a fashion philanthropy gala and to get away from life as I knew it. On my return, I brought back three cups from Starbucks as souvenirs. One day, we were standing in my kitchen, and my partner at the time looked at one of them and said 'sacrilege!' He was invoking some conspiracy theory linking the Starbucks logo to the illuminati, notoriously known to be somewhat of a satanic cult. None of this disturbed me, but the intention of shaming me did. The audacity to enforce a shame on me I did not have in the first place reminded me of my journey with Islam and the constant judgement it came with. I vowed there and then that I would never again make space for religion in my personal life.

I use the terminology offered by the Egyptian-American author and activist Mona Eltahawy to describe myself as being of Muslim descent to point to a history and a position within the social hierarchy, but never an identity. I have realised that people accept religion as inherent, as if we are born with religion. We are not, and we can choose to change our minds about it. It takes a certain level of bravery to assert beliefs that circumvent the hegemony of religion in a society that enforces it. Again, this is the expansion of being that queerness allows. The knowledge that nothing besides a deep humanity is obligatory.

Integral to my evolution was my decision to go back to university after quitting a master's degree in research psychology at Stellenbosch in 2011. I had been writing a proposal for eight months when my supervisor, a white woman, said that I was a bad writer and she couldn't help me anymore.

I moved to Johannesburg and lived and travelled a bit. Then I found a master's programme in critical diversity studies, and I knew I had to pursue my ever-present love for social justice. It had allowed me to reckon with my race broadly and Colouredness specifically among other axes of oppression.

To be able to formulate new understandings of myself in relation to the upbringing I described here has been liberating but also difficult. It is a difficult process to unlearn social conditioning and to bare down under the work required to keep improving. It is unending, taxing work, but the personal rewards for constantly attaining a more profound humanity cannot be underestimated. To experience myself as a being in flux – and be content with it – saves me from the stranglehold of a binary existence. I am content with changing frequently and significantly.

I am also content with letting those who don't want to evolve stay behind. I have in the last ten years had to let go of people I thought would be around forever. One night during our regular bonding sessions, Neil did a tarot card reading for me. He predicted the sale of my family home as well as the end of our friendship. He told me we would break up and stay separated for a period of two years and then reunite only to break up again. This is the perfect summary of our friendship. As instrumental as he was in my life and coming into my queerness, he just didn't know how to be a dependable, genuine friend to me. His love always seemed to grow teeth that wanted to maim me. I have learnt to accept that some people are only meant to teach you a lesson, and when you have learnt it, their purpose in your life is spent. Our relationship has also taught me that maintaining queer friendships can be challenging in a world where we are all vying for visibility. We are set up to compete for scarce resources and to make choices between self-advancement and community.

I have also had to let Tayshira go. We developed a close relationship over the years to the extent that we started mimicking each other. Over time, I realised that it was less that we were closely connected but that I was being controlled. The lukewarm response she gave to my coming-out announcement revealed itself to be a deep need for control over my being. I was always more than happy to centre her in all my decisions and gave her the final word on my appearance. She decided how long my hair should be, when I should shave, what I should wear, and how I should look. It read as concern and care to me in the early years, but I came to understand that what she wanted was to manage my gayness to remain palatable. I was a reflection of her, and she wanted to be able to choose the parts of me that she was comfortable associating with. She wanted the (hetero)normative version of me to make it easier to have me in her life. She doesn't know how to relate to me if I am completely myself with no justifications.

I had spent years trying to convince her that I am an expert on my own lived experience and that her perspective on my life cannot possibly constitute some form of truth. The arrogance enabled by power would not allow her to accept the possibility of being underqualified to make an assessment of a life she has never lived a day of. I had to make a choice between justifying my experiences and looking for approval, and walking away from the symbolic violence of making me labour to prove my experience of oppression. I cannot tolerate anyone who enacts or endorses violence against me in any form.

When writing *Khamr* I could have written a tell-all exposé on my parents and the sometimes-scandalous things I endured growing up. I have gone through many years of introspection to forgive my parents for what they couldn't give me. I have also learnt to forgive them for not giving me the things they could give me because it was simply too hard. Within bounds, of course, I wanted to find a way to write about trauma without sensationalising it. I wanted to demonstrate an understanding of everyone introduced in this book that made them more than just the immediate sum of their actions. We live and survive in contexts that are created by systems, none of which are wholly escapable.

Since the events retold here, I have reckoned with my own experiences of life, and I too understand better how people like my parents made the choices they did. I wanted to write them into being with compassion and understanding without excusing the harm of the choices they made. Since my father's passing in 2018, I have come to understand him better, and to write him down with a sensation-seeking pen would rob both of us of so many opportunities for testimonial justice. It is hard to write about trauma in the context of generations because there will always be another layer to unpack. Sometimes, we really just want a single perpetrator to hold accountable for our pain, and justifiably so. In our case, the debt that was raised in blood centuries ago still haunts us today. Maybe, there is a way for me to write this story and locate it in two generations of trauma, but it would be dishonest.

How we choose to write ourselves into existence has implications for the stories we leave behind. The appetite for our raw trauma – uncensored – is big through the various gazes we are subjected to. It is an act of righteous sabotage against the power of the gaze to contextualise trauma in relation to that very power. When we tell our stories, we must make sure to remind ourselves of where it all started. When we talk about our afflictions, we must show how they came to be. This is not a way of escaping accountability for our own actions but of naming power in all its forms.

This book is about naming power, not only at the level of its mega structures, but also where it has grown tentacles that grip us in self-regulating fear. It is meant to show how power structures mirror and replicate from the top down. How the home is a reiteration of the state. How religion is an accomplice to that reiteration. How we are so easily seduced by the opportunities to exercise power where we can find it.

This story is also a statement about the deleterious effects of othering on people. Loneliness is one. Coming into my own as a critical scholar embodying multiple positionalities has come with loneliness. It's a loneliness more dynamic and plural than the kind that one imagines would keep you sitting in your room all day with nobody to speak to. It is not a loneliness that comes from the lack of contact with people but rather the lack of humanity in our interaction with people.

Day in and day out, having to labour to educate bigots who live to exhaust you with queries asked in bad faith and debates that go nowhere, I have learnt that more people are bigots in one way or another. The percentage of people who are interrogating power and how they are implicated in its structures is very small. Most of us want everything to stay exactly the same. Going out into a world where your existence as a marginalised person is constantly a debate, a survey or an opinion poll is isolating beyond comprehension.

When I first started my critical scholarship, I was convinced that I was going to fight my way to freedom for us all. I was going to channel all the sassiness and rage everyone always had a problem with into the fight against prejudice and oppression. I learnt first that I had a lot of work to do on myself and that it couldn't happen in isolation. That in itself is an alienating process. I realised that I am not the person I thought I was and that I am prejudiced in some ways. I had to learn new ways of being and speaking. When you're the only one doing in and among people who don't see its importance, it gets lonely. I also realised that I could not save the world by fighting every day. That I was not teaching many people but being baited into arguments that wanted to see me disgraced. I had to learn to take care of myself in the midst of a life dedicated to seeing justice for others. It is a lot to juggle, and the journey is hardly ever smooth. Reconciling all these realities makes for a lonely existence. It is lonely to the extent that it is difficult to find a place to breathe and delink from the fight because the work is all around you. It is difficult to just be. Self-care is a deliberate undertaking.

Contradiction comes with the territory. One of the most valuable things I learnt through my critical scholarship is that knowledge is not singular but plural. There are knowledges, and therefore multiple issues can be true at the same time. In the pursuit of truths, we must not aim to be right but to be fair and just. Multiple things can be true at the same time, and sometimes they contradict each other. We exist in constant consultation with our surroundings and are constantly a product of that consultation. The expectation to perform a perfect kind of activism that itself is sanitised of error is unrealistic. We are allowed to learn, grow and change. Contradiction is not uncertainty but reality. The social world we have created is unequal, so when we endeavour to undo it, we are bound to hold conflicting truths. That is a process of enrichment we must allow ourselves to go through. To know multiple things can be true and to live within them simultaneously is far better for solutions than a singular truth can ever be. I have had to learn that contradiction is not dishonesty but rather discovery.

There is a freedom in discovery. In my adult life, I have rediscovered the wonder of exploration I was denied by fear. Not only my own fear, but my mother's fear of letting me explore too far. Although it was meant to protect me, physically, it left a yearning in me intellectually, and it taught me not to try certain things for fear of failure. The association with the creative arts instead of the safer avenue of science was something I avoided for years. Through exploration I found in it the thing I would do for the rest of my life, even though those around me didn't understand it. I have learnt not to do things to be understood. There are those who will eventually come around and those who never will – if they don't understand it, then it's not for them. Through discovery I also realised that I didn't have to be a martyr for other people's desires. I am not here to make sense to everyone but to be present within my own journey of reclamation and self-discovery.

I am reluctant to attach the label of 'activist' to myself, although I am happy to do activism. The label invokes a burden I am not willing to accept. What I hope to do is not persuade people who don't believe in social justice in the first place. I hope to affirm and encourage people who have a love for social justice and true freedom to also use their voices to amplify the message that justice must prevail. Even if they don't use their voices, I want for them to feel seen. I hope to leave behind an archive of knowledge and experience that writes the existence of people like me into history.

I have learnt to seek out people like me if I am to survive the toll a marginalised existence takes on one's mental health. Begging to be accepted in normative spaces is one of the most damaging things we can do to ourselves. No, every now and then we must seek out the people who affirm our realities, and retreat into self-indulgence. It is important to occupy spaces where we don't have to constantly explain and justify our experiences. The daily violence of navigating a society that seeks to annihilate you in various ways does not get easier, and it shouldn't. Finding community with people who are on a similar journey is a part of self-care. I don't have much connection to my birth family anymore because of my unmoving commitment to social justice and what that asks of the people in my life, but I have a chosen family. I have a network of support that is always available to offer a soft place for me to rest when I need it. Some call it an echo chamber, but that concept is generally only applied to justify the constant heckling of marginalised people who refuse to engage with destructive discourses anymore. I protect my peace and make sure that I am taken care of physically, emotionally, intellectually and spiritually.

In light of all that has happened on my journey since coming into myself, this book aims to offer a perspective of experience in an unequal world. It is not an attempt at fixing truth but an invitation to explore it. I am here to make sense of my experience in the world, which is often not talked about through the particular intersections that I have chosen. Mine is not the only experience like this but, having lived it, I know how much shame and fear is attached to attempts to heal from this out loud. We are encouraged to take our confusion and pain into dark rooms to spare the feelings of powerful people who live to see us squirm. This is an account of experience that provides evidence for the existence of people like me, who refuse to accept a shame enforced on me. What I have shared here is not an attempt to disgrace anyone either, least of all my father, but rather one to hold a mirror up to the various societies we create and to interrogate them. It is also an internal critique of the way oppressive systems replicate themselves with marginalised communities who remain silent for fear of further ridicule. That is the point about contradiction and multiplicity. We can be oppressive while being oppressed, and it is on us to live within and resolve that complexity with haste. It was exactly my experience of multiple oppressions that drew me into social justice, and this book is a call for more such stories.

We need our stories, no matter how ugly they are, to rebuild the evidence that was previously erased. It is only when we immerse ourselves wilfully in our multiple unsanitised histories and futures that we can start to construct some semblance of truth.

On Satan and god

The power of words forms an integral part of the brutal history we bear under as Africans, globally. Neutrality of language is a myth. Long before and throughout the material oppression of African people by European and Arab people, language laid the foundation for the worldviews that justified our oppression. In the arsenal of religious weaponry used daily to arrest the senses of people, language was used to subdue us.

Throughout this book, I have played with capitalisation of words in an attempt to invert the power relations embedded in those words. In particular, I have been intentional about the use of Satan and god for a few reasons. The discourse around good and evil in religious discourse, represented by god and Satan respectively, has been undeniably racialised. This is not unique to religion but nevertheless applies there too.

The idea of god has historically been constructed by white religious hegemony to reflect the fantasy of whiteness. The purity, innocence and righteousness of whiteness became a function of godliness and god's likeness. The authority, power and wrath of that same god became a shared characteristic of global whiteness through dedicated racist religious propaganda. I am aware that many people – and followers of religion – have challenged this because it is indeed not true but when I speak of a god in this book, I am speaking of the god that was presented to me under the discursive conditions I have described above. It is this god I would like to strip of his white, cisgender, heterosexual, patriarchal power through diminishing him.

When I speak about Satan, I am speaking back to the historical construction of Blackness and African spirituality as deviant and as proponents of the occult. I would like to denounce the violent and untrue construction of African people as purveyors of dark magic and evil who could only be reformed through accepting the white god described above. I would like to honour the memory of murdered Africans who were slain in the name of a white god they refused to accept and were therefore believed to be possessed by Satan, who was made the scapegoat for justifying white supremacist evil. I would also like to put forward that Satan, I believe, is a metaphor for the evil all people are capable of. Through inverting this historical misrepresentation of Blackness and African spirituality as Satanic, I hope to honour its importance and beauty through language.

When I mention Satan and god in the book, I am still relating the traditional understandings of what those two figures represented to me at the time. When I write them now, I am speaking back to the political constructions they embodied through language – removing the one of political power by writing it all in lowercase and recognising the way in which another was misrepresented by rendering it with an initial capital letter.

This is meant to unsettle and challenge, and it is not a mistake.